THIS IS
EGYPT

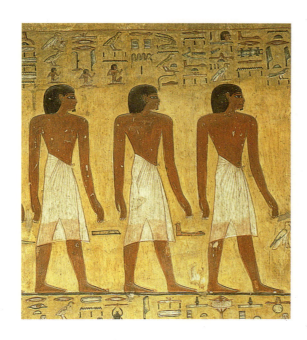

THIS IS
EGYPT

Text by Guy Marks

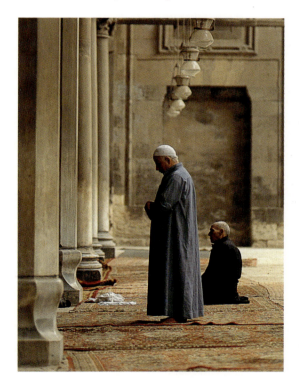

Photographs by James Morris

First published in 1998 by
New Holland Publishers (UK) Ltd
London • Cape Town • Sydney • Singapore

10 9 8 7 6 5 4 3 2 1

24 Nutford Place
London W1H 6DQ, United Kingdom

80 McKenzie Street
Cape Town 8001, South Africa

3/2 Aquatic Drive
Frenchs Forest, NSW 2086, Australia

Copyright © 1998 in text: Guy Marks
Copyright © 1998 in photographs:
James Morris/Axiom Photographic Agency
(except individual photographers as credited below)
Copyright © 1998 in map base artwork: Mountain High Maps™ 1993 Digital Wisdom Inc
Copyright © 1998 in maps:
New Holland Publishers (UK) Ltd
Copyright © 1998
New Holland Publishers (UK) Ltd

Guy Marks has asserted his moral right under the Copyright, Designs and Patents Act, 1988, to be identified as the author of this work.

All rights reserved. No part of this publication may be reproduced, stored in a retrieval system or transmitted, in any form or by any means, electronic, mechanical, photocopying, recording or otherwise, without the prior written permission of the publishers and copyright holders.

ISBN 1 85368 881 9

Commissioning Editor: Charlotte Parry-Crooke
Publishing Manager: Tim Jollands
Editor: Ian Kearey
Editorial Assistant: Rowena Curtis
Designer: Alan Marshall
Cartography: Bill Smuts
Index: Janet Dudley

Reproduction by Pica Colour Separation Overseas (Pte) Ltd, Singapore
Printed and bound in Singapore by Tien Wah Press (Pte) Ltd

Illustrations appearing in the preliminary pages and on the last page are as follows:

HALF TITLE: Tomb painting from the Tomb of Seti I in the Valley of the Kings, Thebes.
FRONTISPIECE: The Hypostyle Hall and Obelisk of Tuthmosis I at the Great Temple of Amun, Karnak.
TITLE PAGE: The Mosque of al-Muayyad, Cairo.
PAGE 4: Coptic church tower at Wadi al-Natrun.
PAGE 5: Camels at the Imbaba Market, Cairo.
PAGE 6: *Felucca* on the Nile near Luxor.
PAGE 176: Schoolgirls in Mut, Dakhlah Oasis.

ACKNOWLEDGEMENTS

The author, photographer and publishers would like to express their gratitude to the following for their generous and valuable assistance during the preparation of this book:

Declan Morton, Hayes & Jarvis (Travel) Ltd • Magdi A. Fatah, Isis Travel, Cairo • Mamdouh Abdel Baith, Marhaba Tours, Sinai • Aladin Kasom, Elephantine Island • Fayek Rezeiky, Luxor • Ernest Alsina, EgyptAir • Hesham Kattan, The Old Cataract Hotel, Aswan • Samir Darwish, Egypt Tourist Office, London • The staff, Abu Chieleb Hotel, Aswan • DDFE Resources

PHOTOGRAPHIC ACKNOWLEDGEMENTS

The publishers and photographer extend their thanks to the following people who kindly loaned their photographs for inclusion in this book:

Didier Brandelet: page 156 (below)
Alex Misiewicz/Axiom Photographic Agency: pages 154 (all three subjects), 155, 157 (above right and below right)
Dorian Shaw/Axiom Photographic Agency: pages 12, 13 (right), 24, 34 (above), 62 (above), 65 (below left), 66 (both subjects), 67 (both subjects), 153 (top), 160 (all three subjects), 161, 162 (all three subjects), 163 (above and below), 167 (above right), 170 (below right), 172 (above)
Lawson Wood: pages 15, 29, 151, 156 (above), 157 (above left and below left), 168 (above), 169 (both subjects)

Contents

Map of Egypt 8

Profile of Egypt 10

The Land 12 • Resources 13 • Climate 14
Wildlife 14 • People 16 • Religions 17 • Language 18
History 19 • Government and Economy 25
Arts 28 • Crafts 31 • Food and Drink 34

Journey through Egypt 36

The Hub of the Nation 36
Giza, Memphis and Cairo

The Nile Delta 60
North to Alexandria and the Coast

Along the Nile to the Valley of the Kings 76
South to Luxor

The Land of the Nubians 106
To Lake Nasser and Abu Simbel

Oases and Sand Dunes 128
The Western Desert

The Red Sea Coast and Sinai Peninsula 150
Bedouin Hinterland and Undersea Paradise

Index 174

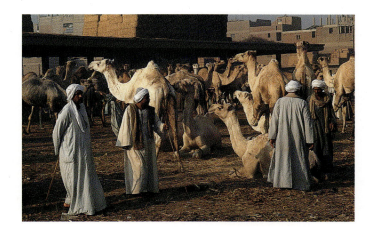

This is Egypt

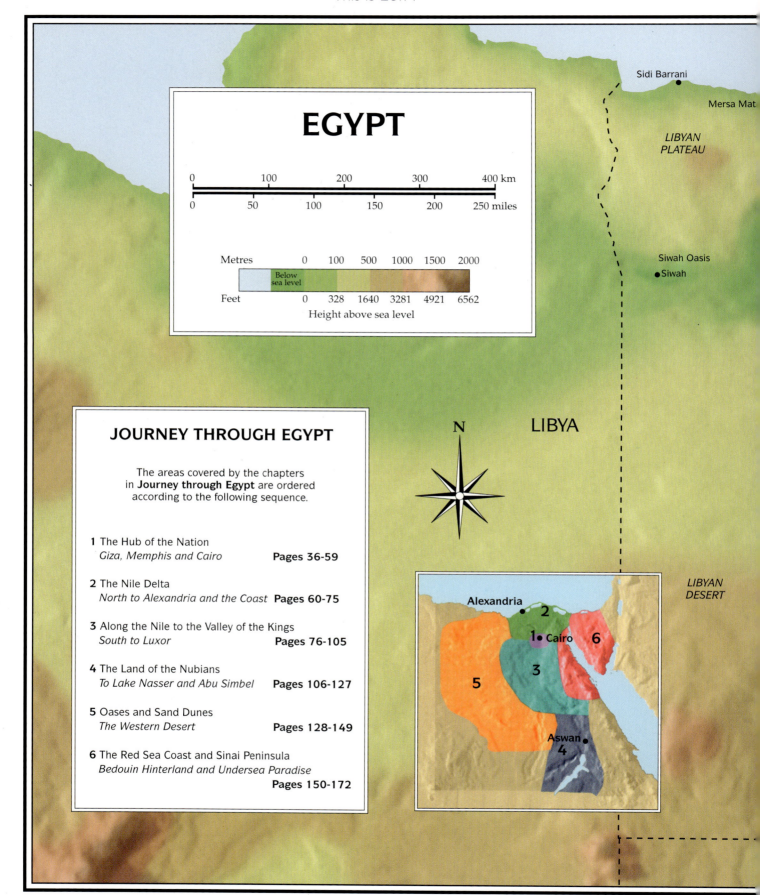

EGYPT

0　100　200　300　400 km
0　50　100　150　200　250 miles

Metres　0　100　500　1000　1500　2000
Below sea level
Feet　0　328　1640　3281　4921　6562
Height above sea level

JOURNEY THROUGH EGYPT

The areas covered by the chapters in **Journey through Egypt** are ordered according to the following sequence.

1 The Hub of the Nation
Giza, Memphis and Cairo　**Pages 36-59**

2 The Nile Delta
North to Alexandria and the Coast　**Pages 60-75**

3 Along the Nile to the Valley of the Kings
South to Luxor　**Pages 76-105**

4 The Land of the Nubians
To Lake Nasser and Abu Simbel　**Pages 106-127**

5 Oases and Sand Dunes
The Western Desert　**Pages 128-149**

6 The Red Sea Coast and Sinai Peninsula
Bedouin Hinterland and Undersea Paradise
Pages 150-172

Sidi Barrani
Mersa Mat
LIBYAN PLATEAU
Siwah Oasis
Siwah
N
LIBYA
LIBYAN DESERT
Alexandria
Cairo
Aswan

This is Egypt

Profile of Egypt

Where Africa rubs shoulders with Asia lies the country where modern civilization began. It cradled the first imperial society, and the monumental achievements of its first rulers are familiar to modern man thousands of years after their lives. Their legacy is in architectural masterpieces such as the great pyramids, and in magnificent monolithic carvings, obelisks and colossal statues. Buildings from every age carry inscriptions in hieroglyphs, pictures and written texts, chronicling this long history. From the earliest times, the comings and goings of great foreign powers have left their mark and enriched the heritage of the country's indigenous people.

Most of the land is made up of vast deserts, scorched by intense sun and hostile to human habitation, where nomads roam and trains of camels are used as reluctant beasts of burden. Through these parched wastelands runs the world's longest river, bringing life and expanding into a fertile delta. To the north, the country's shores are bathed by Mediterranean waters. To the east, it is hemmed by the coral reefs of the Red Sea, where a kaleidoscope of marine life thrives beneath shimmering waters. Beyond the Gulf of Suez, the Sinai Peninsula is the setting for historical Biblical events.

In towns and villages, the smoke of honey-scented tobacco and hot charcoals rises from the snaking tubes of bubbling water-pipes in street-side cafés, and wood clicks on wood in a seemingly never-ending game of backgammon as men in flowing *galabiyyas* sip coffee and watch the world go by. Children play in the streets and a cat darts across the alley, narrowly avoiding the wheels of a donkey-cart; the atmosphere thickens as the smell of incense mixes with the heady aroma of exotic spices.

A vendor hails the traveller: 'Come to my cousin's shop. What are you looking for? I give you very good price because you are my friend.' The game of trade begins, an agile, cerebral dance of bargaining prowess.

This is Egypt.

This is Egypt

The Land

Situated on the north-eastern corner of Africa, Egypt is bordered by Israel to the north-east, Sudan to the south and Libya to the west. It has around 500 kilometres (310 miles) of Mediterranean coastline to the north, and its eastern coast boasts 1,080 kilometres (670 miles) of beaches along the Red Sea. The land area of 997,739 square kilometres (385,127 square miles) consists of 96 per cent desert, making the great majority of the area inhospitable and unsuitable for human habitation.

The lifeline through this desert land is the River Nile, whose waters flow 6,670 kilometres (4,142 miles) from sources way beyond the Egyptian borders, through Sudan from Ethiopia, and Lake Victoria in East Africa. This combination of desert sands with an artery of fresh water has given Egypt an extraordinary contrast of geographical structure.

It is a land with no forests, no permanent pastures and only limited rainfall, yet it manages to support a massive population and was the birthplace of one of the earliest civilizations. The ever-present challenge of taming these geographical contradictions has pushed man's architectural and engineering achievements to new limits, and great projects have changed the very face of the land for over a century.

Throughout history, Egypt has been an important trade route between Asia and Africa. The construction of the Suez Canal, which was opened in 1869, technically severed the land link, which was not restored until 1980, when the Ahmad Hamdi tunnel opened, 16 kilometres (10 miles) north of Suez town, taking vehicular traffic beneath the Canal. The building and opening of the Canal created one of the world's most important maritime routes, linking the Mediterranean to the Red Sea and opening up shipping routes from the North Atlantic to the Indian Ocean.

The damming of the Nile, first with the Aswan Dam and then with the High Dam, is another vast, ambitious engineering project, and the traditional seasons of flooding and drying along the Nile Valley and the Delta have been halted and regulated. The long-term consequences of the damming are only now being appreciated, but the land has been changed forever.

The Delta

Just north of Cairo, the Nile branches into two tributaries, the eastern Damietta and the western Rosetta. In Pharaonic times there were a total of seven branches, but despite the silting of these tributaries the Nile today still expands to a massive delta, a vast flat land riddled with drainage and irrigation canals, that produces a lush, fertile agricultural landscape. The Delta fans out to the Mediterranean coast between the major population centres of Alexandria (population 3,500,000) and Port Said (population 500,000), an area historically known as Lower Egypt. Until the damming of the Nile the Delta was seasonally flooded, and the silt that washed down from Africa's interior replenished the agricultural land. Today, concern over soil erosion along the coast has led to a number of sea defence projects on the northern coast.

The Nile Valley

At the southern tip of the Delta, Cairo and its sister town Giza, on the west bank of the Nile, have an estimated population of 10,000,000, a sixth of Egypt's inhabitants and one of the world's largest conurbations. The first ancient civilizations emerged around the Nile Valley, and it is still home to the majority of modern-day Egyptians. In places the desert sands come right down to the water's edge, but for the vast majority of its course through the country, the Nile provides a green tract of fertility through a scorched landscape. A number of irrigation canals have been built and many more are under construction, taking the life-giving waters beyond the banks to increase the cultivated land. The pace of life along the river is gentle and tranquil, as traditionally styled boats, *feluccas*, ply the waters past green fields where farmers, the *fellaheen*, tend their crops as in centuries past.

The Western and Eastern Deserts

West of the Nile Valley, the desert continues uninterrupted across the continent. Changing only its name, from the Libyan desert in the north-west to the Nubian and Saharan deserts further south, this vast expanse of parched dry land seems never-ending. Palm-lined oases and strange desert geological formations punctuate the land.

PREVIOUS PAGES
Page 10: Feluccas *on the Nile at Aswan.*
Page 11: *The streets of Cairo are often brightened by festival decorations.*

Above: *The interior of the Sinai Peninsula is made up of* wadis, mountains and deserts. *On the eastern side, the desert leads to the spectacular Coloured Canyon.*

PROFILE OF EGYPT: THE LAND

Along the length of the Nile Valley, a system of irrigation canals brings the essential waters of the river to the fields.

For over a hundred years, the Suez Canal has been both an important trade route and a place for fishermen to cast their nets.

So barren and featureless are these vast expanses of sand that international limits have no natural boundaries to follow, and one look at the straight borders to Egypt's west and south demonstrates that these were created by man.

To the east of the Nile lies the Arabian or Eastern Desert. Compared with the Western desert, it is a relatively narrow strip of land, in places just 100 kilometres (62 miles) wide. Here, the landscape has been sculpted by ancient watercourses that carved out their paths and subsequently vanished, leaving dry *wadis*.

The Red Sea Mountains rise out of the desert floor between the river and the shore. Rocks and sand, a sprinkling of boulders and granite chips are scattered at their foothills, spilling over onto windswept plains along the coast.

THE SINAI PENINSULA

North of the coastal resort of Hurghadah, the Red Sea branches to form the Gulf of Suez and the Gulf of Aqabah, two arms of water that embrace Egypt's eastern land mass, the Sinai Peninsula. This, too, is formed from sandy desert, with spectacular mountains dominating the southern interior.

At 2,637 metres (8,444 feet), Mount Sinai is the highest peak in the country, and it is a magical landscape where pink skies emerge from dawn mountain mists. The landscape of Sinai has long been a wilderness of wandering tribes and a place of Biblical prophets and revelations. It is a crossroads of cultures and continents.

RESOURCES

Egypt is fortunate to have a number of natural resources, the most significant being oil and natural gas, which are found around the Sinai Peninsula. They are extracted in large quantities from the Gulf of Suez and offshore deposits in the Mediterranean, as well from the Western Desert.

The country also has deposits of gold, precious stones, iron, manganese, phosphate, tin and uranium. The mining of minerals and fuels has long been established, and development is under way to establish new sources.

However, Egypt's most precious and limited resource is the water of the Nile, which has become essential not only for its role in agricultural production and consumption, but also as a source of hydroelectric power. The first major project to control the waters and provide a broader cultivation base for the growing population came at the turn of the 20th century, when the Aswan Dam was built by the British at the First Cataract, just on the southern outskirts of Aswan. By the middle of the century, however, demand had outreached capacity, and one of President Nasser's first acts as leader was to instigate and commission the building of a new and more efficient dam.

Nasser nationalized the Suez Canal to raise funds and collaborated with the USSR to realize the project. Completed in 1971, the dam created a 6,000 square kilometre (2,316 square mile) body of water named Lake Nasser, the world's largest reservoir. The High Dam has made it possible for thousands of acres of previously barren desert to be reclaimed, and provides permanent irrigation, with the result that yields and harvests have multiplied in this water-managed environment.

The High Dam has also provided a new hydroelectric supply for consumers and industry. While the Aswan Dam still generates power for local consumption, the High Dam, which was fitted with new turbines in the 1980s, produces enough energy to make feasible a giant power project linking Africa and Asia. In this, the largest pylons in the Middle East will stand on the banks of the Suez Canal, linking the supply from Egypt to the networks of Jordan, Syria, Lebanon, Iraq and Turkey.

THIS IS EGYPT

CLIMATE

As one would expect from its geographical make-up, the majority of the country has a desert climate – hot, dry and dusty, with very little rainfall. In the north, Alexandria and the Mediterranean coast enjoy a more temperate, cooler climate, with an annual rainfall of around 20 centimetres (8 inches). This falls mainly in the winter months of November through to February and can produce some heavy downpours, but these become less frequent the further south you go, especially south of Cairo. The spring, from March to April, is relatively mild but brings the *khamsin,* a hot, bitter wind driven across Africa from the Sahara, which is laden with dust and can blow for weeks on end, making life difficult.

Throughout the year Egypt enjoys a consistently long period of daily sunshine: Cairo averages 11 hours in summer and 8 in winter. Temperatures in the north range from daily highs of 18°C (65°F) in the winter to 30°C (95°F) in the summer, while the temperature in the south and desert regions is rarely less than 20°C (68°F) in winter and can soar above 50°C (120°F) in the height of summer. However, the desert areas tend to have large temperature drops at night, and can fall very quickly below freezing in the winter.

THE WILDLIFE

It is impossible to journey to Egypt without encountering the animals that are a part of everyday life as they go about their work in every town and village, and every cultivated field and desert plain. Markets, roads and alleys are filled with donkeys laden with fresh produce. Horses and mules are harnessed to simple carts for transporting goods, or to elegant carriages, the *calèshes*, to carry people.

In the cultivated fields buffalo yield to the yoke, and in the desert reluctant, groaning camels and proud Arabian horses animate the landscape. These animals may be the most immediately noticeable to the visitor, but wherever you choose to look, in the deserts or fertile wetlands, in the mountains, the skies or ocean depths, Egypt teems with wildlife.

The vast and barren Western Desert has a surprisngly varied animal population, which has survived in relative isolation for thousands of years: Fennecs, Rock Hyraxes and Jerboas have all evolved into mammals superbly adapted to their environment.

THE NILE REGION

The Nile Valley and the Delta provide a home for thousands of birds. Some 150 species are native to Egypt, and around another 200 species visit the land seasonally in the course of their migrations. All along the Nile the green fields and riverbanks are populated by egrets and majestic herons which feed on the small fish in the shallow waters and marshlands.

The Nile and the northern lakes of the Delta are home to water birds, such the Great Crested Grebe, Marsh Sandpiper, Eurasian Spoonbill and Pied Kingfisher, that feed on the abundant fish and small aquatic life; in addition, there are nectar-eaters, like the Shining Sunbird, and insect-eaters, like the Little Green Bee-Eater and Golden Oriole. At Birket Qarun near Fayyum, thousands of ducks and wild geese gather each year, and Greater Flamingos can sometimes be seen nesting here.

The people of ancient Egypt held the ibis in high esteem, glorifying it to the extent that it became known as the Sacred Ibis. It was obviously once present in large flocks, judging by the 1,500,000 birds that were entombed in the catacombs of Saqqarah, but has not been seen in Egypt for over 100 years, although it is quite common in parts of Africa further to the south. The only ibis seen in Egypt today is the Glossy Ibis, which passes through on its migratory route.

The Nile is believed to have as many as 190 different species of fish, mainly small minnow-like species, which provide food for the water birds. There are also some more substantial species, such as the Nile Perch and Tilapia. A number of catfish, including the Red-tailed Catfish, feed on the bottom of the silty waters.

The Nile Crocodile has had mixed fortunes in history: it was revered by some ancient Egyptians, but has been feared by most people who come across it. As the human population reached saturation point along the Nile, the crocodile was one of the first victims to fall by the wayside. Considered a dangerous animal, it was killed on sight and all but vanished from the populated shores and irrigated waterways. The creation of Lake Nasser, however, provided a haven far beyond the realms of man's domain, and the crocodile popula-

PROFILE OF EGYPT: THE WILDLIFE

tion has gradually increased south of the High Dam; crocodiles have occasionally been seen very close to Aswan.

THE DESERT REGIONS

Although it is hard to imagine that anything can survive in the unforgiving desert environment, several small mammals, such as Desert Rats, Gerbils and Egyptian Jerboas, make it their home. There are also some considerably larger animals in a few remote places, such as gazelles, jackals and several members of the cat family.

The largest of the native Egyptian cats is the elusive Caracal or Desert Lynx, a permanent resident of the desert regions; the smallest and rarest of the cats is the Sand Cat, which has a covering of hair on its feet to help it to walk on the hot soft sand. The Egyptian Wild Cat or Kaffir Cat is not quite as rare as the Sand Cat, and is similar to today's domestic cat. In fact, the cat was first domesticated in Egypt, and began to be depicted in Egyptian art in around 1450 BC; it is quite probable that the cats seen in every alley and are part of every household have a common ancestry with Kaffir Cats.

Dogs also feature heavily in Egyptian mythology. The packs of wild dogs found in the desert have an uncanny resemblance to paintings and statues of the god Anubis, with distinctive facial features and long, pointed ears. While domestic dogs have evolved into a diverse range of breeds, these desert dogs are probably unchanged from those on which the ancient Egyptians modelled their god.

Among the more unusual inhabitants of the desert regions is the Rock Hyrax which, despite its appearance, is closely related to the elephant. Furry and about the size of a small rabbit, it lives amongst the rocks in the mountain foothills. Another desert mammal, the Fennec, is the world's smallest fox, measuring just 61 centimetres (2 feet), including its tail. Although it is a desert fox, it can be found all over Egypt. Fennecs' small bodies have evolved to help reduce dehydration in the day and heat loss at night; they have large bulging eyes and disproportionately long ears which enable them to hunt at night.

Scorpions and snakes are not uncommon features of the desert, and mongooses can be found preying on snakes. The snakes are also a target for the distinctive Lanner Falcon, which soars high above the desert sands, sharing the airways with a number of hawks and owls, and the Egyptian Vulture.

The astonishing variety of coral reefs and marine life in the Red Sea and the Gulf of Aqabah make diving there an unforgettable experience for beginners and experienced divers alike. The importance of leaving the sites in undisturbed condition is paramount for all visitors.

THE RED SEA

With a spectacular diversity of marine life, the Red Sea is the site of Egypt's only national park, which has been in the forefront of the conservation of coral reef ecology. Ras Muhammed National Park was started in 1983 in a small area around the southernmost tip of the Sinai Peninsula. Since then it has been continually expanded, and now encompasses an area that stretches up to Ras Abu Galum, halfway up the Gulf of Aqabah.

What makes this area so special, and such a magnet to divers from all over the world, together with the sites further south along the Red Sea coast, is the pristine condition of its coral reefs. A range of different hard and soft corals live here, including table Acropora, Stylophora, Porites, Goniopora, fire coral, cabbage coral, spiky elkhorn coral, gorgonian sea fans, Xeniid soft corals and castle-like bommies. Habitats range from single species stands to complex compounds of biodiversity that coexist in equilibrium. At its most simple level, this variety of life is supported by a rich concentration of plankton, all of which provides a perfect habitat for a plethora of reef fish, ranging from Clownfish and brightly coloured Parrotfish to stingrays, groupers and moray eels.

In addition to the catalogue of tropical coral dwellers, several different sharks cruise the waters, including Hammerheads, Greys, Whitetip and Blacktip reef sharks, and sometimes Whale sharks. Large fish are plentiful, especially in the deeper waters: Barracuda and Surgeonfish, schools of snapper and the giant Napoleon Wrasse can all be found, and Hawksbill Turtles, octopus, cuttlefish and squid are in abundance. Dolphins are frequently seen.

Perhaps the strangest of the sea creatures to be found in the waters around the country is the Dugong. A relative of the Manatee, it is a member of the sea-cow family, feeding on beds of seagrass. It is little studied and not often seen, but when it does appear it is the highlight of any experience of the underwater world of Egypt.

THIS IS EGYPT

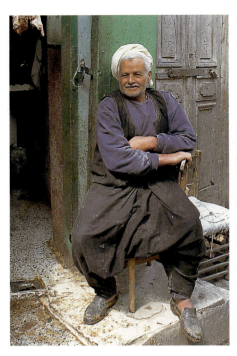 

The standard garment for men in rural areas, and also found to a lesser extent in the towns, is the galabiyya, *a flowing robe (below left). Rosetta was an important trading post under the Ottomans, and it is still possible to see men there who wear the distinctive 'Turkish' clothes that were introduced in that era (far left). Bedouin tribes were the original inhabitants of Sinai, and Bedouin women continue to wear traditional head coverings (left).*

The Nubian people of the south of Egypt are physically closer to sub-Saharan Africans than the more northerly Arabs, who have Semitic origins (below).

THE PEOPLE

Egypt is home to more than 60,000,000 people, nearly double the population in the 1970s. Although this growth rate has slowed a little, it is still causing a major population explosion, which has been one of the country's most pressing problems. To add further difficulties, 98 per cent of the population lives within the 4 per cent of land area that is not desert. This has put considerable pressures on the major cities and habitable land, and the Delta and the Nile Valley have become one of the most densely populated areas in the world.

The long history of civilization in the Nile area has created a culturally rich and distinctive people. Invaders and colonizers have occupied the country over the centuries, but each has added to the culture without diluting the identity of the people, the majority of whom come from four distinctly different origins. The largest group are Afro-Asian Arabs, who can claim an ancestry stretching back through the ages to Semitic origins or, more precisely, to the Hamites, the tribe of Ham. Thought of simply as Egyptians, they represent the vast majority of the population. They are the modern-day people of the cities, and the fellaheen who continue to farm the fertile land as they have done for centuries.

The Bedouin Arabs were originally nomadic people of the desert, and still keep to many of their traditions. City life does not appeal to them, and although some try to maintain a nomadic life, most have found places to settle in the deserts and oases of the Western Desert, Sinai Peninsula and along the Red Sea Coast. They have a deep empathy with the desert which has forged their characters. They are expert camel herdsmen and desert trackers, able to survive where others would falter from lack of food and water.

The Berbers similarly favour the desert regions and inhabit the same oases towns in the Western Desert as the Beœouins. They are North African Arabs, typically of Libyan heritage. In the area around Siwah, a small minority group of Berber Arabs descended from the tribes of Zanatah have closely guarded their traditional roots, maintaining a Berber dialect and traditions, and keeping their cultural heritage distinct from the wider Egyptian community.

The south of Egypt and the area straddling the border with Sudan was once known as Nubia. Its inhabitants, the Nubians, are a much darker-skinned people and quite different from other Egyptians, having more of an African than a Middle Eastern heritage. Nubia survived as a distinct land for thousands of years, yet was all but lost in the 1960s when the Aswan High Dam was built. As Lake Nasser spread across the desert and submerged the traditional Nubian homelands, along with many of the monuments that were a link to their ancient culture, the Nubians became a displaced people and some 800,000 were resettled in the area around Aswan. The islands of the First Cataract now make up a centre of the Nubian population; Elephantine Island alone has a population of 2,200 and can be regarded as the modern-day capital of Nubia. The Nubians are a proud people and seem to take a fatalistic attitude to the loss of their traditional lands. They make the best of their life around Aswan, and have become known for their business skills, as well as for building and sailing *feluccas*.

ISLAM

When Islam was first brought to Egypt in the 7th century, it was still a religion in its infancy. At the age of 40, the Mecca-born prophet Muhammad received his calling to Allah in AD 609 and founded the Islamic faith, instigating the scriptures of the holy text, the *Quran*. The Muslim general Amr conquered the Byzantine army of Egypt in AD 636, and the seeds of Islam were sown in the country. The religion was slow to take a hold, however, and it was not until the 11th

For Muslims whose professions mean that they cannot be always in the same place at the times for devotions, a makeshift prayer mat can be substituted for the real thing.

century that it became the majority religion in Cairo. Nearly two more centuries elapsed before it was accepted as the majority religion in the country.

Today, around 90 per cent of Egyptians are Muslims, most of whom follow a traditional form of Islam known as Sunni, with a small minority of Bohra and other non-Sunni sects also represented. Cairo is one of Islam's most important theological centres: al-Azhar University is a study centre for Islamic scholars from all over the world, and the Rector of al-Azhar is an influential figure on global Islamic religious issues. Some Muslims would welcome a change to a more religiously fundamental way of life in Egypt, forsaking Western influences and adopting religious rather than civil laws. This attitude has unfortunately led at times to terrorist attacks on non-believers by groups of Muslim fundamentalists, one of the chief concerns of the Egyptian government.

Islam plays a vital part in the lives of its followers throughout the whole country. The architecture of every city, town and village immediately conveys the Islamic heritage, with the tall minarets above the ubiquitous mosques dominating the skylines. The regular call to prayers from the *muezzin* echoes across the communities, who wake each day to the words, 'It is better to pray than to sleep', the first of five calls to prayer each day, the others being at noon, late afternoon, sunset and night.

Although most mosques incorporate segregated areas for women to pray in, these are not universal, and sometimes just men attend the mosques. However, prayer can just as easily be carried out in the home or wherever the devotee happens to be at the given time, and it is quite normal for a shopkeeper to interrupt his trade, place a prayer mat on the floor facing Mecca, and prostrate himself before Allah. Most Muslims make the effort to attend the mosque itself on Friday, the holy day of the week. The ninth month of the lunar year is a time for fasting and abstinence, called Ramadan, when Muslims are required to fast between the hours of sunrise and sunset, a practice which is intended to evoke religious contemplation and bring a closeness to God.

CHRISTIANITY

Christianity was introduced into Egypt by the Apostle Mark in AD 45. Although he made a number of converts, the faith here remained an underground movement for some time, and the Egyptian Christians developed a belief in the absolute divinity of Jesus, questioning the human aspect; the faith became known as Coptic Christianity. As in their other conquered territories, the Romans saw the Christian influence in Egypt as a disruptive threat to their authority. The culmination of their persecution was in the late 3rd century under the rule of Diocletian, when thousands of Copts were slaughtered; the Coptic calendar takes its base date from the massacres of AD 284.

Despite such opposition, Christianity spread throughout the Roman Empire and gradually attained acceptability. In AD 313 it was legalized by the Edict of Milan, and a

THIS IS EGYPT

The official title of the Coptic Patriarch, Shenude III, is Pope of Alexandria and Patriarch of the See of St Mark; the seat of the patriarchy is in Cairo.

number of monasteries were built in Egypt, with St Catherine in Sinai, the Red Sea Monasteries and the monasteries of Sohag and Wadi al-Natrun among the most famous. This still did not bring peace to the Copts, as the Byzantines followed a different order of Christianity and there was always a conflict between the two practices. The Copts were expelled from the Orthodox Church in AD 451 and looked to the Patriarchate of Alexandria for leadership. The friction between the Coptic Egyptians and the Byzantine overlords played a part in the eventual rise of Islam: many Copts converted to Islam, and others saw the new religion as an opportunity to remove the oppressive Byzantine rule.

Despite the massive popularity of Islam, there is still quite a strong Coptic Christian community in Egypt today, accounting for the majority of the non-Muslim population. In addition to the Copts there are small minorities of Roman Catholic, Protestant, Greek and Armenian Orthodox Christians in the country, although this is due to more recent immigrations for the most part.

The long tradition of Christianity in Egypt has left the country a rich cultural legacy. In addition to the monasteries, which are in varying states of use or repair, there is still a Coptic quarter in Cairo where the history of Egyptian Christianity can be followed through the exhibits at the Coptic Museum. There are a number of active churches in Cairo and in other major towns in Egypt.

JUDAISM

Just as Christianity in Egypt preceded Islam, Judaism preceded Christianity. According to the Old Testament, it was to Egypt that the Jews migrated in a time of Middle Eastern famine, and the book of Exodus records their subsequent departure in search of the Promised Land. Moses is said to have seen the burning bush and received the Ten Commandments at Mount Sinai, and this sacred history led to the building of St Catherine's monastery at Sinai, still a major pilgrimage site for both Christians and Jews.

Jews returned to Egypt during Ptolemaic times and settled in Alexandria; St Mark's first convert to Christianity was one such Alexandrian Jew. Although many Jews converted to Christianity, a strong Jewish community continued to thrive, living alongside Christians and sharing their mutual dislike of

Intricate, carved Islamic inscriptions on a wooden lintel over a door are a common feature in Al-Qasr in the Dakhlah Oasis.

Roman rule. These Jews were known for their skills as silversmiths and goldsmiths as well as their business and banking activities. The community seems to have survived as Egyptian-Jewish until European colonial times, when European Jews came to Egypt. Many Jews migrated to Israel after its foundation in 1947, but relationships between the two countries were fraught with problems: the Suez Crisis of 1956 and the Egyptian-Israeli war of 1967 made it almost impossible for Jews to stay peacefully in Egypt. Today, there are only a few hundred Jews left in the entire country, and the Ben Ezra Synagogue in Old Cairo is one of the last Jewish buildings to survive as a reminder of a long legacy.

LANGUAGE

The Arabic that is spoken almost exclusively throughout the land is in fact a colloquial modern version particular to Egypt; it is a dialect of the official written, broadcast and religious Arabic language of Egypt, which is also understood in all Arab countries.

Since the days of colonial rule, both French and English have been widely spoken by educated Egyptians. Some government decrees are published in French as well as in formal Arabic, and both Cairo and Alexandria have a wide circulation of French-language newspapers. There are also small communities of Greeks and Armenians in some of the major towns, who have brought their own languages with them, and small communities in the Western Desert oases still maintain their traditional Berber language.

One of the languages used by the ancient Egyptians is also referred to by experts as 'Egyptian', but this is now extinct in its original form. It was recorded in hieroglyphs and papyrus manuscripts, and is thought to have originated during the 3rd millennium BC. During the 2nd century AD this form of Egyptian developed into the Coptic language, which continues to be used for religious ceremonies within the Coptic Church.

The History of Egypt

The history of Egypt spans 5,000 years of civilization and untold eras of human development before that, and is inextricably linked with mythology and ancient religious beliefs. Relics of ancient times still dominate the modern landscape alongside the wonders of the recent technological age. The names of great pharaohs, kings and gods, together with warriors, peace-keepers and modern political leaders have become a part of Egypt's great heritage and culture. It is impossible to visit the country without at some point becoming immersed in the intricacies of this remarkable history.

It is clear from archaeological findings that man settled in the area around the Nile as the surrounding country turned gradually into desert. Over thousands of years, hunter-gatherers became settled farmers, fishermen and herdsmen, and socially cooperative communities started to develop. These communities expanded to form two separate lands, Upper Egypt, in the Nile Valley as far as the Delta, and Lower Egypt, in the Delta itself. The people of Upper Egypt worshipped the god Seth, the god of chaos, and those of Lower Egypt worshipped Seth's nephew Horus, the falcon-headed god, the son of Isis, the great goddess of magic, and Osiris, the lord of the underworld and resurrection.

The Early Pharaonic Dynasties

In about 3000 BC, a king called Menes founded a city at the junction of Upper and Lower Egypt. This city, Memphis, united the two lands and created an empire, thus becoming the world's first imperial city. This event was the start of the 1st Dynasty (each dynasty being a hereditary line of rulers), and records show that even at this time, efforts were being made to include Sinai in the Egyptian territories.

By the time of the 3rd Dynasty (c.2650-2575 BC), a level of organization within the empire enabled the construction and development of monumental architecture. This was the start of an era known as the Old Kingdom; relics from this age include the Step Pyramid at Saqqarah, built by the architect Imhotep for King Zozer, during whose rule the empire worshipped the supreme sun god Re.

The Step Pyramid Complex of the 3rd-Dynasty King Zozer is one of the world's most ancient monuments, and is thought to be the first constructed of stone throughout.

The 4th Dynasty (c.2575-2465 BC) saw the empire branching out to campaigns in neighbouring countries and a continuation of architectural progress. The last three kings of the dynasty, Khufu (Cheops), Khafre (Chephren) and Menkaure (Mycerinus), were responsible for the construction of the Great Pyramids of Giza. The kings of the 5th Dynasty styled themselves as sons of the gods and introduced religious texts to their pyramids. They started to share their power with high-ranking officials, as can be seen by the emergence of tombs for nobles, as well as those for royal families. This subdivision of government led to the rise of new power centres within the empire, and by the end of the 6th Dynasty and the death of its last Pharaoh, Pepi II, around 2152 BC, disputes between the factions had brought the empire into civil war and dissolution, marking the end of the Old Kingdom.

The period that followed brought a succession of kings and dynasties about whom very little has been discovered in detail. What is clear is that the north and south of Egypt were at loggerheads and that the troubles were not brought under control until the beginning of the 11th Dynasty (c.2050 BC), when Mentuhotpe II founded a new centre of authority in Middle Egypt at Thebes, near what is now Luxor. He was able to reunite the empire and began a 300-year period of prosperity known as the Middle Kingdom. During this time many monuments still extant were constructed and there was artistic, economic and commercial development on a hitherto unseen

The actual and symbolic uses of the Solar Barque, possibly the world's oldest boat, discovered in a pit just beside the Pyramid of Khufu at Giza, are still a mystery.

This is Egypt

Akhenaten's switch of religion was mirrored by an emphasis on more naturalistic forms of sculpture and painting.

scale. The capital was moved back to Memphis, and then transferred to Fayyum. However, a period of poor harvests and political pressures after 1800 BC brought the empire under pressure, and the stability of authority ebbed. Small principalities and kingdoms emerged, and eventually invaders took control of the country, bringing the Middle Kingdom to a close at the end of the 15th Dynasty in around 1640 BC.

For the next 100 years princes known as Hyksos ruled over Egypt. They seem, however, to have made little impact on the existing culture and may have encouraged traditional Egyptian values rather than introducing their own beliefs. Egypt was never united under their rule, and there was a constant regional challenge for power. Eventually Kamose, the king of Thebes, emerged as the most powerful force and besieged the Hyksos capital in the Delta. The 'foreign' rulers were expelled by Amosis in c.1550 BC, from which time the empire began one of its greatest eras.

The New Kingdom

The period from 1550-1070 BC covers an era of expansion and prosperity: the empire developed international power and recognition, and the rulers acquired wealth and economic stability, using this wealth to erect great monuments, temples, mausoleums, and public and state buildings. Many of the ancient Egyptian sites that attract thousands of visitors today were originally constructed in this period, and the pharaohs that built them are the ones whose names have lived on.

The colossal ruined statues in the Great Temple of Amun at Karnak bear witness to the devotion of the New Kingdom pharoahs to this deity.

The first of the 18th Dynasty pharaohs was Amosis, followed by Amenophis I. In religion, the emphasis moved towards the deity Amun, who was the supreme creator god at Thebes, the capital of the New Kingdom, where a number of temples were erected to honour Amun. There was also massive expansion of the temple complex at Karnak, originally built in the Middle Kingdom period. Existing faiths were incorporated into the Amun deity to create incarnations such as Amun-Re, the king of the gods. Amun and his consort Mut, depicted with a vulture head-dress, and their son Khonsu, the moon god, became known as the Theban Triad of deities.

Tuthmosis I expanded the empire by taking possession of Nubia. This not only brought in revenue of precious metals and tradable commodities, such as ivory, ebony and gemstones, but also provided the Egyptians with a workforce of Nubian slaves; the royal tombs in the Valley of the Kings were started during the rule of Tuthmosis. On his death his daughter Hatshepsut became ruler; she instigated new construction on the West Bank at Thebes and had a spectacular mausoleum and temple built at Deir al-Bahri.

The empire was further expanded and enriched by the pharaohs that followed her: Tuthmosis III, Amenophis II and Tuthmosis IV all played their part in furthering the Egyptian boundaries by force or politically motivated marriage. Meanwhile the era of construction continued, reaching a new peak under Amenophis III, who built the temple complex at Luxor and was responsible for the Colossi of Memnon. These statues of the Pharaoh, which were classed as one of the Seven Wonders of the ancient world, stand on the west bank at what was once the entrance to a mortuary temple, now long-since disappeared.

The worship of Amun was interrupted when Amenophis IV and his wife, Nefertiti, switched their allegiance to the sun disc Aten. In order to mark this, Amenophis changed his name to Akhenaten and founded a new capital at Tell al-Amarnah. Both the capital and the state religion, however, were short-lived, and when Tutankhamun was brought to the throne as a boy king in c.1333 BC, he was persuaded to return the capital to Thebes and to discon-

PROFILE OF EGYPT: HISTORY

tinue the worship of Aten. These differences between the Amarnans and the Thebans came to weaken the empire, with internal instability and the loss of some territory.

The 19th-Dynasty Pharaoh Ramesses I recaptured the lost territories and restored the empire to its former glory. His successors Seti I and Ramesses II continued the trend and were responsible for another era of monumental and artistic construction, notably the Ramesseum at Thebes, the temple at Abydos and the Sun temples at Abu Simbel.

THE LAST OF THE PHARAOHS AND PERSIAN RULE

There was no sudden end to the great Pharaonic dynasties; instead, they dwindled over a considerable period. The beginning of their downfall was at the end of the reigns of the Ramessean Pharaohs of the 20th Dynasty (c.1196-1070 BC), when Ramesses XI allowed the administration of the kingdom to be divided once more into Upper and Lower Egypt. The divided kingdom fell prey to foreign invaders from Libya, whose kings ruled Lower Egypt in the 22nd Dynasty. Unity was temporarily restored by the Nubian kings of the 25th Dynasty (c.770-657 BC), but they were unable to regain the power of the former empire.

Further invasions came first from the Assyrians and then from the Persians. The Persian invasion of 525 BC introduced powerful new emperors, Cambyses and then Darius I, who ruled unsympathetically over the land. The Persians lost control of the country and were replaced by native pharaohs for the period 404–343 BC. Starting with Amyrtaeus and ending with Nectanebo II, these 28th, 29th and 30th Dynasties were constantly under threat from the Persians and formed an alliance with the Greeks to help maintain their sovereignty. Although defeated by the armies of Artaxerxes III in 343 BC, the Persians were reinstalled for another brief period.

GRECO-ROMAN OCCUPATION

Persian rule in Egypt was brought to a sudden end in 332 BC, when their empire was

One of the most famous ancient landmarks in Alexandria, Pompey's Pillar actually has no connection with that ruler, but was built six centuries later, in honour of Diocletian.

conquered by Alexander the Great. He quickly established his administration and founded the city of Alexandria, but at his death, only nine years later, the empire he created was immediately carved up and shared out amongst his generals. One of these, a Macedonian called Ptolemy, became Egypt's new ruler and the era of Greek occupation began.

Egypt prospered from the cultural integration and development of Hellenistic arts, architecture and philosophy, and yet managed to maintain the style and grandeur characteristic of the ancient Egyptian forefathers. Greek became the official language, and a library housing works translated into Greek was built in Alexandria. A Jewish community was encouraged to settle in Alexandria and what was to become Cairo. Meanwhile, in the south of the country, cult temples to Pharaonic gods were built in places such as Edfu and Kom Ombo.

Ptolemaic Greek rule lasted for 300 years, surviving until Roman influence dominated the known world. The last of the Ptolemies was Cleopatra VII, who managed temporarily to harness Roman power by romantic affiliations, first with Julius Caesar and then with Mark Antony. However, the Emperor Octavian sent forces to annex Egypt to the Roman Empire; Cleopatra and Antony committed suicide in 30 BC, and Egypt became a province of the Roman Empire.

In terms of the country's development, Roman rule brought prosperity in the same way as under the Greeks. Egypt became a grain exporter to the Roman Empire and an important link in the developing trade routes. Roman rule coincided with the rise of Christianity, first brought to Egypt in AD 45. Over the next 250 or so years the Coptic Christians in Egypt became more prominent, much to the disgust of the Roman rulers. In AD 313 Christianity was made the official state religion of the Roman Empire by the Emperor Constantine, but nearly 80 years later the Empire split into two separate power centres. Rome remained at the head of the Western Empire, but Egypt fell under the control of the new eastern capital of Constantinople (now Istanbul), the centre of what was to become the Byzantine Empire.

The Byzantines' orthodox Christian beliefs were essentially different to those that had become developed by the Coptic Christians in Egypt. The religious conflict that ensued between the people and their foreign rulers was to continue throughout the next two and a half centuries of Byzantine rule, despite the nominal acceptance of the same basic faith.

THE RISE OF ISLAM AND THE CRUSADES

In AD 638 the Arabs defeated the Byzantine army and set about taking over the Empire. In 640 they started a successful campaign in Egypt, and by 642 had captured the capital at Alexandria. General Amr established a new capital at Fustat in the vicinity of what is now Cairo.

Just as the Roman Empire had had its internal disputes, the Islamic Empire was rife with sectarian power struggles. From 658 Egypt was ruled by the Ummayad dynasty from Damascus, but in 750 power transferred to the Abbasids of Baghdad, who ruled the country for about two centuries, although there was a brief period of independence when an administrator called Ibn Tulun was sent to Egypt in 868. He declared independence, establishing a new city at a site just north of Fustat called al-Qitai and building one of the largest mosques in the world. His family's rule only lasted for 37 years before the Abbasids reimposed their command in 905. The mosque fell into disrepair and was not restored to its present glory until the end of the 13th century. The Ikhshidid dynasty was installed by the Abbasids in 935 and was given a modicum of independence. After just 30 years, however, the country fell into a state of political instability.

Taking advantage of this instability, the Fatimids arrived in Egypt from Tunisia in the west in 969, expanding their empire across North Africa and the Middle East. The Fatimid commander Gohar founded the new city al-Qahirah and within it the mosque and Islamic school of al-Azhar; today these remain as the city of Cairo and al-Azhar University. For the next 150 years the Fatimid Khalifs ruled over their empire from the Egyptian capital. Their reign was largely a time of prosperity for the country with the exception of 11 years under the Khalif al-Hakim, who appears to have been completely deranged, imposing extraordinary laws and persecuting women; following his mysterious disappearance in 1021, a small following proclaimed he would be reincarnated as the Messiah.

During the Fatimid era the Europeans started their military campaigns to reinstate Christianity throughout the Arab World, and in particular to take Jerusalem from the Muslims. These campaigns, the Crusades, started in 1097, and saw Jerusalem captured in 1099. Over the next 50 years Lebanon and all of Palestine were taken into Christian control, and the threatened Fatimids opted for a policy of cooperation rather than risk the loss of Egypt. The Muslim Seljuk dynasty in Syria saw this as considerably weakening their own position and sent an army to take Alexandria under the command of Salah al-Din, who founded

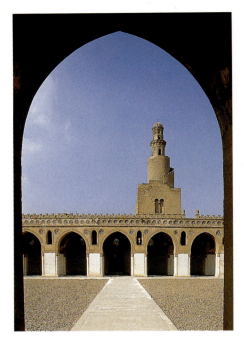

The great Mosque of Ibn Tulun, the oldest in Cairo, was started in 876; the spiral staircase on the outside of its minaret is the only one of its kind in Egypt.

his own dynasty in 1171 after the death of the last Fatimid. Known as Saladin in the West, he took the title of Sultan and set about reclaiming the Muslim lands. He fortified Cairo after a Crusader attack in 1176, building what is now the Citadel. The Crusader campaigns were protracted, but Saladin gradually won back the territory and finally recaptured Jerusalem in 1187, five years before his death. His Ayyub dynasty continued to rule Egypt until the middle of the 13th century.

The Mamluks and the Ottoman Empire

The success of the Muslim Empire under the Abbasids, the Fatimids and the Ayyubids had long been dependent on mercenary soldiers; young boys from the Turkish-speaking regions were bought as slaves and trained to become a mobile warrior force. These soldiers, known as Mamluks, played a large part in the Crusades, and their leaders gained a certain amount of power within the political structure of the country. Their chance came when the last of the Ayyubids married a Turkish-speaking slave girl, Shagar al-Durr, who took the seat of power

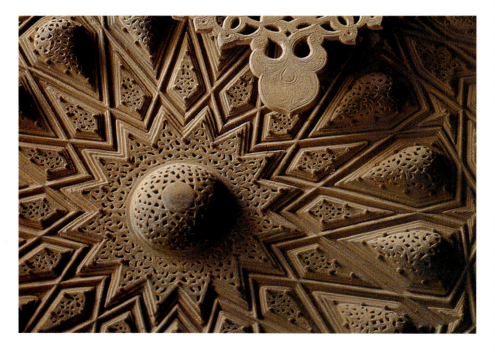

The arrival of the Muslims brought new modes of artistic expression to Egypt; one typical style is geometric decoration based on star shapes, found in metal, wood and stone work.

after his death in 1249. She was obliged to take a husband, but their mutual distrust of one another led to his murder, followed shortly by her own assassination. By this time the military leader Baybars had attained a high position under Shagar al-Durr, and he was quick to take over, beginning 267 years of Mamluk rule.

The first Mamluk dynasty was the Bahri Mamluks, who continued the long-standing Muslim campaign to repel the Crusaders and routed them from their last stronghold in Acre in 1291. Theirs was a constructive era both physically and politically: architectural development produced distinctive buildings and mosques such as the Sultan Husan, el-Zahir and Qayaun mosques in Cairo, and new trade and political relations were established on an ever-widening international network, particularly with European powers and the Hapsburg Empire.

The greatest threat to peace, both for the Bahri dynasty and the Burgi Mamluks who succeeded them in 1382, was the persistent desire of the Mongols to expand their territories. In 1387 the Mongols once again threatened to invade Syria, having been defeated and repelled from the country a century earlier by the Bahri Mamluks. This time the military defence was to cost the country dear, and brought the Egyptian economy into a desperate state. During the next 100 years the economy never fully recovered enough to make Egypt an important power, and when the spice traders discovered a new route to the east around Africa's southern Cape, the country's finances were dealt a further blow.

Meanwhile to the north, the Ottoman Turks had been gaining a foothold in Europe and the Middle East, and when they attacked the Mamluk territory in northern Syria, Egypt was in no shape to mount a successful defence. In 1516 the Sultan Qansuh was killed in battle and his successor Tuman Bey, the 47th Mamluk Sultan, was defeated and executed within the year. The Ottoman Empire remained in absolute power for the next 272 years. Governors or *pashas* administered the country as a province, sending back taxes to the imperial purse. Although the Ottomans were the overlords, the Mamluks still held many positions of authority. Their warrior heritage was never forgotten, and they remained the core of the Egyptian army; this power even enabled them sometimes to depose Ottoman governors whose decisions were not to their liking.

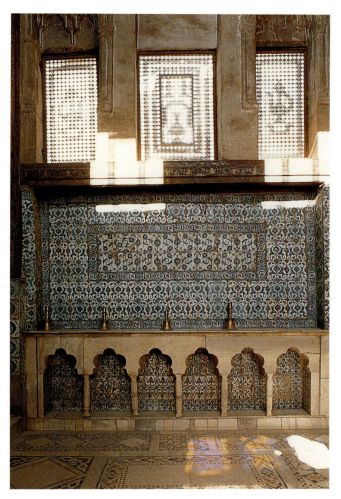

Despite political instability, many 17th-century merchants prospered through trade with Europe, and built impressive dwellings such as the Bayt al-Sihaymi in Islamic Cairo.

A struggle for authority emerged between different families of Mamluks in 1556, and the Ottomans seized the opportunity to play off one faction against the other to weaken the Mamluk stronghold. By the end of the 16th century civil wars were being fought between the Mamluk factions, allowing the Ottomans to take greater control over their Egyptian empire. The country's economy suffered badly from the increased taxes that were levied to fund the various armies. Through the 18th century European trading partners imposed import restrictions to aid their own economies at Egypt's expense, and economic decline set in. Consecutive years of low waters in the Nile led to poor crops and caused famine and disease. By the late 18th century the country was in a state of chaos.

At this time the struggle for power between the great European powers of Britain and France was at its height, and Napoleon decided to take Egypt as a French colony, securing trade routes to the East with the intention of countering the British Empire. He landed in Alexandria in 1798 and occupied parts of the Delta and the capital, but he never managed to hold any territory in the south of the country, and after his naval fleet was sunk by Nelson in 1799, Napoleon fled back to Europe, leaving his army under the command of General Klèber. When Klèber was assassinated, his successor, General Menou, had great ideas for Egypt, but was in command of an army who wanted only to return to France. The British were keen to get the French out of Egypt and formed an alliance with the Ottomans. The resulting Anglo-Ottoman army routed the French from Alexandria in 1801.

The Ottomans were reinstated as governors of Egypt, but both they and the Mamluks had lost any loyalty and support from the Egyptian *fellaheen* over whom they had jointly ruled for centuries. Out of the chaos emerged a young Turk, Muhammad Ali, at that time the commander-in-chief of the Albanian forces, a mercenary wing of the Ottoman army, who made his way to power in 1805 and introduced radical changes to the country.

Regarded as the founder of modern Egypt and the state system, Muhammad Ali spent the first years of his rule putting down opposition and crushing Mamluk dissent.

His final clear-up operation was a massacre of 470 Mamluk leaders and their principal lieutenants, who were ambushed at a ceremony at the Citadel to which he had invited them. The greatest achievement of Muhammad Ali's 44-year rule was to Egyptianize the army and governmental authorities. With the armies depleted and the Mamluks wiped out by his own hand, he needed to replenish the forces and set about training the *fellaheen*, improving the country's education and technical knowledge to do so.

Muhammad Ali's effective army, still an instrument of the Ottomans, was sent to expand the empire. Muhammad's son Ibrahim controlled the army but wanted independence from the Ottomans to create an Egyptian State. The success of his armies was seen as a threat to the European powers and led to a series of treaties, alliances and trade agreements involving the Greeks, Russians, British and Austrians. The Ottomans supported some Egyptian campaigns and yet were threatened by Egyptian dominance in others. Muhammad Ali's armies were repelled from Syria and his power was much reduced.

Ibrahim died before his father, and his son Abbas was the next ruler. Abbas wanted Ottoman rule to be reinstated, and did little to improve the country. He was assassinated in 1854, and his uncle Said, Muhammad Ali's son, came to power. In his youth Said had formed a friendship with Ferdinand de Lesseps, and on attaining power Said granted Lesseps a concession to build the Suez Canal. This was, however, not completed until 1869, in the reign of Said's nephew Ismail.

A British Protectorate

The debts and treaties that had been established to build the canal were extraordinarily disadvantageous to Egypt and her economy. Ismail was forced to sell out to the British in 1875, giving them a substantial interest in the Suez Canal Company. Ismail's successor Tawfiq came into conflict with the British, and eventually became con-

Originally established in 1859 as a camp for workers building the Suez Canal, Port Said grew in population and importance as a major maritime city during the second half of the 19th century.

trolled by them: Sir Evelyn Baring (later Lord Cromer) was installed as the British Consul-General, and British officials were placed in prominent positions within the Egyptian government. To all intents and purposes Egypt became a British colony, although at the time it was referred to as a 'veiled protectorate'. Cromer managed to establish an economic base for the country, but his presence met opposition from a nationalist movement under the leadership of Mustafa Kamil.

Even though the British had control of the country, Egypt was still officially part of the Ottoman Empire. When World War I broke out, Turkey sided with Germany, creating a political anomaly in Egypt. The British formally declared Egypt a British Protectorate, to look after their interests and maintain control of the Suez Canal. The British High Commissioner, Sir Reginald Wingate, had ultimate power over the Egyptian head of state Fuad, who was Ismail's sixth son. All these factors fuelled an anti-British campaign by nationalists, who eventually achieved their aim when Britain abolished the protectorate in 1922. Egypt was independent for the first time since the Pharaonic dynasties, and Fuad assumed the title of king. The British maintained certain interests in the running of the country and retained the Suez Canal. Fuad's son Faruq brought the British occupation further to a close, but still allowed them to administer and defend the Suez Canal Zone.

Because of its continuing ties with Britain, World War II saw Egypt become a British base once more. Under General Montgomery, Britain's Eighth Army fought Rommel's Africa Korps in 1942 in the desert at the battle of Al-Alamayn, just 64 kilometres (40 miles) from Alexandria. This ended in a decisive victory for the British, and was a turning point in the campaign in the Western Desert. Having re-established their presence in Egypt, the British were reluctant to fully withdraw after the war, as they still had control over the Suez Canal, but in 1947 they came again into conflict with the nationalist and fundamentalist movement, the Muslim Brotherhood.

Revolution – the Republic of Egypt

In May 1948 the state of Israel was created at the expense of Palestine, causing an uproar and military invasion from Egypt, Iraq, Syria and Jordan. The United Nations intervened, and the treaty of 1949 redefined the disputed borders, with the Arabs repulsed from Israel but with Gaza left under Egyptian control.

Throughout this the British were still in collaboration with Faruq, in that they maintained control over Suez, but the Israeli conflict did little to quell the growing amount of

PROFILE OF EGYPT: HISTORY

anti-British feeling. Faruq was forced to abdicate in 1952 after a revolution by Free Officers who seized power and installed themselves in government. The Revolutionary Command Council (RCC) had effective control, abolishing the monarchy, dissolving the political parties and revoking the then Constitution. Egypt was declared a republic in 1953, and after some internal wrangling within the RCC Gamal Abd al-Nasser became acting head of state in the following year, although he was not declared President until 1956.

One of Nasser's first acts was to get the British troops out of the Canal Zone in 1954. For the time being, though, he still allowed the ownership of the canal, and therefore the revenue generated from it, to remain with its foreign shareholders. When international loans, needed to build the Aswan High Dam, were vetoed by the USA, Nasser nationalized the Suez Canal and formed an alliance with the Soviet Union. In response, the British and French contrived with the Israelis to instigate an invasion of Sinai in October 1956. British troops were sent into Port Said and the ensuing conflict was only settled by UN intervention.

The canal was reopened under Egyptian control. In an attempt to widen Egypt's political standing, Nasser then formed an alliance with Syria in 1958, and the two countries temporarily took the title of the United Arab Republic (UAR), a title that Egypt retained even after the dissolution of the alliance in 1961.

Peace was not to last long, as Israel threatened to invade Syria in 1967. Sinai was at this time under UN monitoring, but Nasser sent in troops with the intention of cutting off the Israeli supply line to the port of Eilat. The Israelis responded quickly and brought the war to a conclusion in six days, destroying the Egyptian Air Force while it was still on the ground; they then permanently occupied Sinai and the Gaza Strip.

Egypt Today – the Arab Republic of Egypt

After Nasser's death in 1970 the new president, Anwar el-Sadat, broke ties with the

The establishment of the Republic of Egypt in the early 1950s meant the end of centuries of colonial rule. In Tanta in the Nile Delta, photographs of popular heroes of the country are displayed in public.

Soviet Union and jailed many of Nasser's top aides. In 1971 he restored Egypt's official name to the Arab Republic of Egypt, and called his actions 'the corrective revolution'. He implemented a new and revised Constitution, and in 1972 expelled all Soviet military advisors. Sadat responded to the continuing conflict with Israel. In 1973 Egyptian forces crossed the Suez Canal into Israeli-occupied Sinai in an attempt to recover the territory lost in 1967. As a result UN forces were sent in, and a buffer zone was set up between the two countries.

Sadat's policy of foreign investment, introduced in 1974, began to bring prosperity and opened up a real opportunity for Egypt to become strong. There were, however, still problems of food shortages and the ever-present threat from Israel. In 1977 Sadat saw a way to improve the country's international standing with the West, and signed a treaty with Israel under American supervision. The Camp David Agreement brought an end to the conflict, gave Israel recognition from Egypt and gave Egypt the territory of the Sinai Peninsula. The last Israeli forces withdrew from the Sinai Peninsula in 1982.

This peace agreement with Israel did not find favour with other members of the Arab world, and in particular it aroused Muslim fundamentalist opposition in a minority group within Egypt itself. Fundamentalists assassinated Sadat during a military parade in 1981, and Husni Mubarak became the new President. Under Mubarak, Egypt has continued to strengthen relationships with Israel, and at the same time has improved diplomacy with other Arab states – the President encouraged the making of a peace settlement between Israel and the Palestine Liberation Organization (PLO), and also attempted to settle the Iran-Iraq crisis of the 1980s. During the Gulf Conflict in 1991, Egypt sided with other Gulf states in the formation of an Arab regional security force that was instrumental in the liberation of Kuwait.

Government and Economy

The government of the Arab Republic of Egypt is constructed in accordance with the Constitution implemented by Anwar el-Sadat at the beginning of the 1970s. This provides for an executive President who is the Head of State and answers to a single legislative chamber of 454 members, the People's Assembly, of which 10 of the members are personally appointed by the President. The People's Assembly is elected by universal suffrage; the President is then nominated and elected by a two-thirds majority by the People's Assembly for a term of six years. Elected after the assassination of Sadat, President Husni Mubarak is at time of writing still the Head of State, having been re-elected for a third consecutive term in 1993.

The government is overseen by a Council of Ministers and headed by the Prime Minister. The President is responsible for appointing and dismissing all ministers. The assembly can require a minister to resign if it passes a motion of no confidence in him. If, against the President's wishes, a vote of no confidence is passed against the Prime Minister, the matter can be put to a referendum. There is also a Consultative Council called the *Majlis as-Shoura*, which consists of 210 members, of whom 140 are elected and 70 are appointed by the President.

This is Egypt

Built to replace the original Aswan Dam, the High Dam is over two miles long. It has enabled the annual flooding of the Nile to be controlled completely, and its hydroelectric power station has greatly increased Egypt's power supply.

For administrative purposes the republic of Egypt is divided into 26 governorates (*muhafezate*), each of which has a governor (*muhafez*) and a governor's council. Most of the governorates are made up of a city and its suburbs, or are part of a territory that comprises a chief town and main district. Five of the governorates are towns – Cairo, Alexandria, Port Said, Suez and Ismailiyyah; eight of the governorates are in the Delta region – Behira, Damietta, Kafr al-Shaykh, Garbia, Dakhlia, Sharkia, Tahrir and Qalyubia; a further eight are in Upper Egypt – Fayyum, Beni Suef, Giza, Minya, Asyut, Sohag, Qena and Aswan; and the remaining five governates are what are called frontier areas – Red Sea, New Valley, Matruh, North Sinai and South Sinai.

During the course of Sadat's government six main political parties took shape, and these remain the major influences today. They are the National Democratic Party (NDP), Socialist Labour Party (SLP), Socialist Liberal Party, New Wafd Party, National Progressive Unionist Party and Democratic Nasserist Party. At the time of writing, the National Democratic Party is in the seat of power, after it was re-elected in 1995 by an overwhelming majority. The Head of Government is Kamel Ganzouri, who was elected Prime Minister in 1996.

Economy

Sadat introduced a more democratic and tolerant government and set about reducing the role of the state in the economy, implementing an open-door policy, the *infitah*, to try to introduce foreign investment and encourage private investment. However, on his accession to the presidency Mubarak inherited a country in the clutches of poverty, with a massive international debt. The recent history of war and peace with Israel has had a vast influence on the nature and expenditure of foreign aid, and the population explosion has put further pressure on the economy.

Torn between Arabic and Western cultures and loyalties, Mubarak introduced a programme of modernisation and economic reforms, aimed at taking the country away from state socialism towards a market economy. The initial reforms did nothing to help the economy in the 1980s, when unemployment rose to well over 20 per cent; it was only in the second half of the 1990s that these reforms started to take effect. Billions of dollars of world debt, particularly to the USA, were allowed to accumulate, and the problem was further compounded by the return of Egyptian nationals who had been working abroad. In 1983 over 3,250,000 Egyptians were working in the Gulf States and Libya and sending money back to Egypt. A downturn in the oil industry reduced the number of workers required in the Gulf States, and in 1985 the Libyan government issued an order prohibiting the employment of Egyptian workers. This act alone saw 500,000 return to Egypt, and a further 250,000 returned from Iraq in 1986 when restrictions were imposed on how much money they could send home.

The Gulf conflict of 1990–91 brought another 1,000,000 refugees back from Iraq and Kuwait and simultaneously wiped out Egypt's tourist industry, at that time a major source of income. Egypt's allegiance to the actions of the USA during this conflict, however, resulted in a considerable reduction in debt. By the mid 1990s there was still poor economic growth, although inflation had been brought down to its lowest level for 40 years. The privatization programmes were slow to get off the ground, and the deregulation or removal of trade barriers to encourage foreign investors was limited. Unemployment was still rife, and around a quarter of the country's 60,000,000 inhabitants were living on less than US$35 per month.

In 1996 Prime Minister Ganzouri was appointed with a mandate to rejuvenate the economy and renew the impetus of reform. He continued the work to meet the various targets that had been laid down by the International Monetary Fund and, remarkably, these targets were more than being met by the spring of 1997. Foreign creditors now see Egypt as a donor-friendly debtor with a substantial change in position from the early 1990s, when there was a high prospect of default on the massive debt. The biggest challenge now facing Egypt is how to manage its sudden economic success in an effective way.

Industry and Energy

The Egyptian textile industry has the potential to make a big impact on the country's economy, but it is in drastic need of reform and is plagued by out-of-date technology coupled with artificially manipulated raw

Profile of Egypt: Economy

material prices. Despite this need for reform, Egypt still exports 50 per cent more cotton as the USA; textiles account for 16 per cent of exports and make a large contribution to the economy. The cotton crop yields some 400,000 tons, which is subject to a government minimum producer price. Unfortunately for the textile industry the price is set above the world cotton price, which makes it highly uncompetitive. In an effort to stem foreign imports, the government has in some cases been selling cotton to local spinning companies at a price which undercuts the world market price.

This situation, together with a tendency for manufacturers to look outside the country for a consistent and less expensive source of materials, has resulted in Egyptian cotton stocks being sold at a loss and a conflict of interests between public and private sector weaving industries. The textile manufacturers have the advantage of low labour costs, skilled manpower with decades of experience and the ability to produce a high quality product. Some companies are taking full advantage of this, but others are suffering from overemployment and are using good cotton to make bad products.

Egypt is going through a gradual process of industrialization due to its availability of natural resources, electrical power from the Aswan Dam and a low-cost labour force. Apart from textiles, Egypt produces building materials such as cement, plastics as an oil-based product, electronic products, automobiles and chemicals.

The country has a large production of oil, natural gas and electricity. In 1996, oil exports brought in a revenue of US$1.6 billion (10^9) from a production of 880,000 barrels a day. New finds continually compensate for declining levels at the older reserves. There are seven state-owned refineries which process some 60 per cent of the crude production, but this cannot meet the domestic requirement for oil products, and the balance has to be imported.

Natural gas reserves are estimated to be 1 trillion (10$_{12}$) cubic metres (35 trillion cubic feet), and this could well prove to be the energy source of the future. A large investment is required to establish commercial extraction and pipelines, and negotiations for international trade in gas are already well under way, with Turkey as the main trading partner. Electricity is produced from the Aswan Dam and the High Dam, which generate more than enough power for industry, agriculture and domestic and commercial use. Some electricity is also produced from wind field power generators and from solar energy.

Agriculture

The Nile Delta and the Nile Valley are the main cultivated areas, representing just a tiny fraction of the land area but attracting the vast majority of the population, 40 per cent of whom are involved in farming in some form or other. Farming practices have been centred around small, family-owned holdings since the feudal system was abolished and private holdings were reduced by decree, first to 80 hectares (197.6 acres) and then further to 20 hectares (49.4 acres). The main export is cotton, although agricultural commodities, such as potatoes and other vegetables are also sold on the international market. Although Egypt produces much maize, wheat, rice and sugar cane, it still has to import a considerable percentage of its foodstuffs.

A number of irrigation programmes have increased the area of land under cultivation and its productivity. The most ambitious current project aims to divert 10 per cent of the water flow from the Nile to the New Valley. This is intended to increase agricultural production in the area around the four oases and allow for the resettlement of 3,000,000 people to the area within the next 20 years.

The Suez Canal

The revenue generated from tolls on vessels and cargo passing through the Suez Canal provides an important source of income for Egypt's economy. After clearing the sunken vessels that had blocked it after the 1967 war, the Canal reopened in 1975 to enjoy a steady increase in traffic, peaking in 1982 with a daily average of 61.8 vessels. The Canal still provides up to a third of Egypt's revenues, but has seen something of a decline in recent years.

The development of larger oil tankers that cannot use the canal fully-laden has made it imperative for much cargo transportation to take alternative routes. Among these, the land routes across Israel have improved, with some cargo being unloaded in Eilat and hauled by road to Ashdod for reloading. Oil pipeline projects have also

In the Fayyum region, irrigation canals have been in use since the time of the Middle Kingdom – over 3,000 years – and huge water wheels are still used to move the waters diverted from the Nile along their course.

improved, and here Egypt seems to be in competition with itself. The Suez-Mediterranean (Sumed) pipeline allows ultra-large and very large crude carriers to discharge oil at Ain Sukhna, the terminal at the Gulf of Suez, pass through the Canal empty, and reload the crude oil at the Mediterranean terminal near Alexandria. Dredging is underway to allow for these bigger vessels to pass through the Canal fully laden, but it is estimated that this will take until 2007 to complete.

TOURISM

The tourist industry was hit very badly by the Gulf conflict in 1990–91, and has been further wounded by terrorist action from Islamic fundamentalist militants, aimed directly at tourists. Despite this, in 1996 close to 4,000,000 visitors went to Egypt, expanding an industry whose income rose to in excess of US$3 billion. As a source of foreign currency income, tourism is second only to remittances from Egyptians living abroad. The tourist industry has been the single biggest winner from the economic reforms described above. The private sector has taken a considerable interest in the industry, and the World Bank has approved large loans and equity investments for infrastructural improvement to developments in tourist areas. At the same time the government has budgeted some US$22,000,000 for the promotion and marketing of tourism.

THE ARTS

In the relative isolation of Egypt's early history, its people developed and nurtured artistic and architectural skills which were to astound peoples from all over the world as they made contact with this remarkable land. Egypt is still regarded as one of the cultural centres of the Arab world, with a long history of civilization which precedes most other cultures.

LITERATURE

A specifically Egyptian form of literature, as distinct from classical Arabic literature, only

The Sphinx and the Pyramids at Giza are the most familiar images of Ancient Egypt, inspiring paintings, novels, poems and literally millions of photographs, and have become essential destinations for tourists from all over the world.

started to develop at the beginning of the 20th century. Before then, there was no tradition of novel-writing along Western lines; in Egypt, as across the Middle East, 'literature' encompassed epic and romantic poetry, folk-tales and stories based on Koranic narratives, often recounting the lives of the prophets, and scholarly works on history, philosophy, geography, biography and science. Even among all this, Egyptian writing played a small part, as most literature originated elsewhere in the vast Muslim Empire or among the Arabic communities in Western Europe, notably in Spain and Sicily.

The single most famous literary work to be associated with Egypt, and to be considered Egyptian by modern-day scholars, at this time was *The Thousand-and-One Nights* of Harun al-Rashid, also known as *The Arabian Nights*. Originally based on Persian and Indian stories and legends, this was first drafted by al-Jahshirayi in the 10th century. Its final form was written down in Egypt in the 14th century, from where it became a success both throughout the Middle East and, later, in Western Europe.

Classical Arabic literature was added to and expanded throughout the Mamluk and Ottoman eras; the European tradition of novel-writing, in which social issues were addressed and everyday speech was used, made its mark on Egyptian thought and writing during the period of successive French and British occupation in the 19th and early 20th centuries. One of the earliest novelists to write in this vein was Muhammad Hussein Haykal, who published a romantic but socially observant book entitled *Zaynab* in 1913. He was soon followed by Taha Hussein, a blind intellectual who pursued a career as an Arabic novelist, and Tawfiq al-Hakim, who became regarded as one of the formative figures of Egyptian literature, portraying his visions of the country with an autobiographical account of his first 30 years. Other writers, such as Yahya Haqqi and Yusuf Idris, have furthered the genre with short stories.

The acknowledged modern master of Egyptian literature is Naguib Mahfouz. His early works were based on Ancient Egyptian history, but with the publication of *A New Cairo* in 1949, his writing moved into a new era of current social and political comment that has defined his style since. In over 40 novels – the most famous being *Midaq Alley* – and 30 screenplays, he has used colloquial Egyptian Arabic to describe the lives of the Egyptian urban underclass, to the extent that he has been dubbed 'The Scribe of Cairo'. The Cairo Trilogy brought his talents to the attention of an international readership, and in 1988 he received the Nobel Prize for Literature.

Another novelist read widely both inside and outside Egypt is Nawal el-Saadawi, a feminist psychiatrist whose works look at the role of women, not just in Egypt but also in the wider Arab world. However, her struggle to bring women's rights to international attention has put her at loggerheads with the establishment; like other prominent 'realist' Egyptian authors – even Mahfouz – not all her works are currently available in her native country.

Music and Dance

As with literature, Egypt's long tradition of music and dance has been expressed largely within an Islamic framework. Although the song of the *muezzins* and *munshids*, who recite religious verse in the mosques and at festivals, is an evocative sound of everyday Egyptian life, in the early days of Islam music was regarded as one of the *malahi*, or forbidden pleasures. From the 9th century, however, court patronage began to play an important part in the development of new melodies and songs, which were accompanied by instruments such as the *nay* (flute), *oud* (lute), *qanun* (zither), *rebab* (bowed lute) and *tar* (tambourine), all of which are still played in performances of traditional or classical Egyptian music.

During successive centuries, Persian and Moroccan music and lyrics were added to the native version, and the resultant pan-Arabic music remained relatively unchanged until the Napoleonic invasion in the late 18th century, when European influences first began to make their mark. Western orchestral instruments were introduced, originally to play European Classical music, but were soon used in a synthesis of instrumental styles that is still popular today. In the 19th century, Abdu el-Hamuli made the first compilation of classical Egyptian music and dance, and in the 20th century, the first singer to capitalize on the boom in music brought about by the age of mass communication was Om Kolthum, who became a national figure known as 'The Mother of Egypt'. Her music, in the classical Egyptian vein and based on poetry and operettas, used both traditional instruments and full orchestral backing, and this tradition has been carried on by Abd el-Halim Hafez and Farid el-Atrach, among others. At the same time, music schools were founded, some to teach only the classical traditions and others to work with Western styles.

The 1980s and 1990s have seen the gradual development of two styles of more modern music, *al-jeel* and *shaabi*, which blare from both legal and pirated cassettes across the country and dominate the listening habits of Egyptian youth, throwing up their own superstars. *Al-jeel* combines modern electronic music with the beats and rhythms of the Nubian and Bedouin traditions and has non-contentious lyrics. *Shaabi*, on the other hand, is given to politically and socially provocative messages and has become a music of the poorer classes, particularly in urbanized areas.

Traditional and folk musics are still living traditions, and can be heard at the *moulids* and other festivals. The Bedouin and Nubian areas have their own distinctive forms of music, with sparser melodic accompaniment and more emphasis upon solo and ensemble singing; to Western ears, Nubian music sounds Far Eastern rather than Middle Eastern.

Again due to the Islamic influence, social dancing in Egypt has long been largely confined to religious festivals, weddings and private parties, and even at these the dancing is segregated – men dance in public and women among themselves in private. Despite this attitude, the minority Sufi Muslims consider dance to be a spiritually enriching exercise, and encourage their adherents to use it as a way of attaining closer communion with God; the ecstatic, frenzied dances of these 'whirling dervishes' are known over the world.

The tradition of belly-dancing is in conflict with Muslim fundamentalist views on promiscuity, but it is still a largely accepted dance form, much as in the days of the 19th and early 20th centuries, when it was a standard feature of any evening's entertainment. Shows are put on in many of the large hotels and resorts in the major towns and cities, often performed by Western dancers, although Fifi Abdu and Leila Murad are two of the most famous 'Oriental' dancers today. They attract large audiences, not just of Egyptians but also of tourists and visitors from the West and from other Arab states.

Architecture

The ancient Egyptians were remarkable in their innovative architectural design and construction; the very scale of their monumental structures poses questions yet to be satisfactorily answered about the methods of construction in a pre-technological age. Given that they achieved such wonders as the pyramids in a time when the rest of the world was barely at the stage of simple construction, they have to be considered the founders of architectural engineering.

The pyramid developed from early versions constructed in the 3rd Dynasty (2649–2575 BC); among the surviving

In Sinai, groups of Bedouin musicians travel from festival to festival, to play the folk music of their people and keep their traditions alive in a time of great changes.

examples of this early form are the Step Pyramid at Saqqarah and the Collapsed Pyramid at Maydum. Architectural technology was refined in the 4th Dynasty with the Bent Pyramid at Dahshur and brought to its finest expression with the Great Pyramids of Giza, which were finished c.2528 BC.

The temple architecture characterized by the temples at Thebes was a product of a far later time. Although the temple complexes were continually added to by successive generations of pharaohs with their own designs, they were constructed broadly during the New Kingdom (1550–1070 BC), the era when colossal statues were introduced, such as the Colossi of Memnon at Thebes (c.1350 BC) and the Ramesses II Colossi at Luxor and Abu Simbel (c.1260 BC).

When Egypt came under the rule of the Ptolemies in 304 BC and later the Roman emperors in 30 BC, new forms of architecture were introduced. The Greeks and Romans combined their own architectural styles with the designs they encountered at the ancient Egyptian sites and a new era of monumental architecture evolved, much of which involved modifying existing temples as well as constructing new sites. After the legalization of Christianity, monasteries and Byzantine basilicas sprang up in Sinai, Wadi al-Natrun, the Red Sea Coast and even as far south as Aswan, where St Simeon's monastery, overlooking the First Cataract, was built in the 7th century.

The arrival of Islam in AD 642 heralded what was to become a new dominant feature for the skyline of every town and city in the land. The architecture of mosques developed into magnificent buildings complete with domes and minarets. The oldest surviving example of a minaret in Egypt today, and possibly the first to have been built, is the unique minaret with an external staircase spiralling to its zenith at the mosque of Ibn Tulun in Cairo, which was started in 897.

A characteristic feature of the Islamic influence was the introduction of ornate and complex carvings to decorate buildings. The representation of living things is frowned upon for mosque decoration; however, this did not suppress the inventiveness of architects and masons, who used the prohibition to develop an artistic use of geometric designs and arabesque calligraphy.

The Islamic style of high-ceilinged buildings centred around a courtyard, archways, intricately carved wooden screens, lattice windows and balconies was reflected in the domestic architecture of the Mamluk era of the Middle Ages, from about 1250. Some of the finest examples of this style of Islamic architecture can be seen in the area known as Islamic Cairo.

Mud bricks have long been the staple material used for rural village architecture and peasant dwellings. Flat roofs are standard in most of the country; in the Delta region these are often thatched to give extra protection from the rain. In adverse climatic conditions, the lack of stability of these mud-brick buildings means that they are in a constant state of change, from being eroded to being repaired and rebuilt, giving them an unfinished appearance.

Sculpture and Painting

The huge range of sculpture and painting developed in Ancient Egypt – from fully three-dimensional sculptures and colossi, through painted high reliefs and deep engravings to flat, two-dimensional artwork – is known throughout the world, and has been a magnet for generations of art-lovers, historians and Egyptologists.

Even before the Pharaonic period, there was a clearly defined tradition of sculpture and painting; unearthed artefacts of the pre-Dynastic inhabitants of the Nile include brightly painted pottery and small sculptures made out of clay or carved from ivory and bone. The carved slate known as the Palette of King Narmer is the most historically significant early Ancient Egyptian sculpture. Dated to around 3100 BC, it depicts the victory of the Upper Nile over the Lower Nile, which paved the way for the foundation of the world's first imperial society. Over the course of the Pharaonic dynasties, this society used every form of artistic skill to record both great events and everyday life along the Nile. Its picture writing evolved into hieroglyphs, the precursor of the written word.

Sculpture also changed, moving from the idealized anatomical representations of the early Dynasties to a more subtle, naturalistic portrayal of human and animal figures. The sculptures that have come down to us today range from tiny figurines and animals, often found in tombs, to the gigantic statues and bas-reliefs that were intended to give their subjects a god-like appearance. Vivid and highly coloured paintings adorned the walls of every tomb and temple, and were set down on papyrus scrolls. Like all Ancient Egyptian art, their purpose was religious,

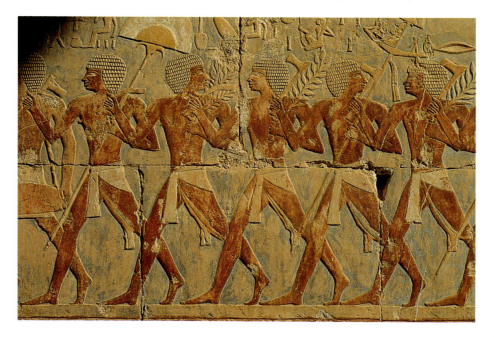

The painted reliefs in the Tomb of Queen Hatshepsut, on the West Bank of the Nile at Thebes, portray life in the 13th century BC with astonishing vividness and clarity.

PROFILE OF EGYPT: CRAFTS

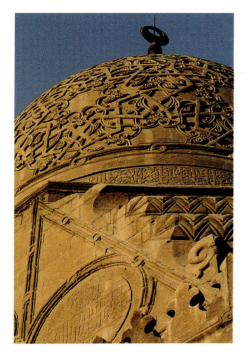

The carving on the dome of the Mausoleum of Sultan Qayt-bay in Cairo is one of the masterpieces of Islamic architecture.

based around worship and the afterlife, but at the same time the artists incorporated a wide range of expression of the diversity of life. Impressive examples of tomb painting can still be seen today in the Valley of the Kings and Valley of the Queens; among the most well-known paintings are those in the Tomb of Nefertari, which show the queen playing a board game, *Senet*, and worshipping the sun god.

Painting and sculpture had been combined from the earliest times, and when other crafts, for example gilding, were added, the decorative arts produced such stunning, world-famous pieces as the death mask of Tutankhamun (in the Egyptian Museum in Cairo) and the painted head of Nefertiti (in the Egyptian Museum in Berlin), as well as countless other equally impressive funeral pieces and sarcophagi.

Having reached such a sophisticated level, sculpture and painting remained comparatively static for many centuries – even in the time of the Greek and Roman Empires, Egyptian art drew on the style of Ancient Egypt. Motifs, reliefs and paintings of narrative scenes were all repeated and copied ad infinitum, and techniques such as bronze casting were used to continue this process. The one major exception to the Ancient style was Coptic religious art, which developed during the Byzantine period and was influenced equally by Byzantine and Egyptian peasant styles. Both ancient and modern Coptic sculptures and paintings present bold, naïve and highly stylized representational images with strong links to Orthodox Christian iconography.

The 20th century has seen relatively radical developments in contemporary art, originally influenced by Western painters but slowly finding an authentically Egyptian style. After World War I, the colonial atmosphere in Alexandria encouraged painters such as Mahmud Saïd and Muhammad Naghi to experiment with Impressionist and Expressionist techniques in their landscapes and portraits.

In 1946 a group of prominent artists, including Hamdi Nada and Abdel Hadi al-Gazzar, formed the Contemporary Egyptian Art Group. This was aimed at bringing the themes of the country's heritage and rich local culture into a modern medium, and the art thus generated has become an increasingly appreciated genre since the 1960s, with artists such as Gazbia Serri, Abdel Wahab Morsi and Wahib Nassar among the best-known painters.

CRAFTS

The Egypt of 5,000 years ago was a highly civilized society with a passion for the aesthetically pleasing. So much of Ancient Egyptian history has been preserved and recorded by the handicrafts that have survived the ravages of time, that we are able to get a clear idea of how many crafts still commonplace today have been developed over thousands of years.

COTTON AND TENT-MAKING

Egypt's role as a major cotton producer has established a number of crafts which make use of cotton textiles, including clothing and house- and tableware. One craft is peculiar to Egypt. Throughout the Islamic world tents, or marquees, are used for religious and ceremonial gatherings and for festivals, and Egyptian tent-makers produce highly ornate canopies decorated with intricate arabesque designs, which are created by cutting patterns out of contrasting coloured cloths and then sewing them together in a distinctive type of appliqué. The tent-makers of Cairo have further diversified this craft, and now use their traditional skills to produce other objects, such as cushion covers and wall hangings.

The restored Galal House is one of the many buildings in Rosetta which display the use of bricks as decorations, a practice dating from Ottoman times.

At a Government-run training school in Al-Khargah, girls are taught to weave wall hangings and woollen rugs. The revival of this ancient craft began in Al-Harraniyyah, near Giza, and its popularity has led to schools and workshops being set up around the country.

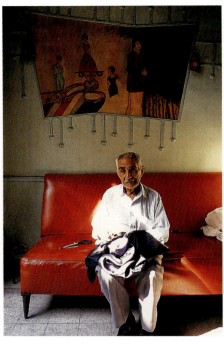

Taking advantage of Egypt's role as a producer of textiles, the tailors of Cairo offer their customers a very fast service.

Glassblowing

Although glass has been manufactured in the Middle East since about 3000 BC, the technology to make it into containers does not appear to have been established until about 1500 BC. In the Greco-Roman era a glassworks at Alexandria was the known world's most important production centre, and when the Phoenicians, who occupied an area in Palestine and Syria, invented the practice of free-blowing glass in the 1st century AD, the Egyptians were quick to develop the new skills.

Little has changed over the centuries, and the skilful craft of glassblowing is still practised in Egypt. In addition to storage jars, decanters and drinking vessels, the most obvious examples of handcrafted glasswork can be seen in the numerous shops which sell delicate glass perfume bottles that have been blown into wonderfully extravagant designs.

Perfume

From inscriptions and paintings on the walls of ancient Egyptian monuments, it is clear that the use of perfume has been an intrinsic part of social status since early history, when perfumes were used to anoint the living and embalm the dead. The fragrances were extracted from flowers, as well as from natural resins, as is demonstrated by a mural at the temple at Edfu, which depicts perfume extraction from the Madonna lily.

In more recent times the city of Banha, about 50 kilometres (31 miles) north of Cairo in the eastern Delta, has become the centre of the perfume industry. The farmland here is rich and fertile, and vast fields of roses are grown and harvested to produce attar of roses, the aromatic floral extract which is the raw material for the perfume industry.

Gold, Jewellery and Metalwork

The wealth of fine jewellery and ornaments brought up from the tombs of Ancient Egypt shows that the Egyptians were pioneering goldsmiths. The most famous of these early works is the death mask of Tutankhamun, which is superbly handcrafted in gold and inlaid with turquoise. Gold was reserved for the monarchy and nobility, and was probably available in quite large quantities – Tutankhamun's solid gold coffin weighs over a tonne – from mines in the Eastern desert.

Each new era of international influence over Egypt has been reflected in the styles adopted in the production of ornamental metalwork. The skills of early craftsmen became developed and diversified with the introduction of less expensive metals, and a walk through any bazaar of modern-day Egypt will reveal dozens of craftsmen working away with brass and copper, as well as jewellers working with silver and gold. The finished articles range from simple engraved trays fashioned from brass, to complex and intricate silver jewellery inlaid with precious and semi-precious stones.

Over the past couple of decades Islamic art in Egyptian jewellery and metalwork has been brought to a new zenith. Azza Fahmy, perhaps the most accomplished master gold- and silversmith, and her sister Ranada have devoted many years to the study of Islamic art in metalwork, and have reintroduced many of the past styles and skills by recreating antique pieces. They have gained international recognition for their designs and have developed a new market for ornamental metalwork and jewellery, to the extent that their customers include royalty and prominent world figures.

Profile of Egypt: Crafts

The backstreets and alleys of Cairo are home to a huge number of craftspeople. The objects produced in what appear to be cramped and chaotic conditions include everyday items, such as scales for use in markets and the home (above left), *and more specialized items, such as engraved calligraphic lettering* (above right).

Once the items have been made, they may not have to travel far to be offered for sale, often lumped together in a bewildering array of seemingly disparate objects (right).

Papyrus

Papyrus sheets are made by splitting and joining stems of the papyrus plant, and have been used as surfaces for writing and drawing since about 2400 BC. Those papyrus rolls that have survived since the time of the Pharaohs are among the most important sources for details of both historic events and everyday life in Ancient Egypt. Because the rolls were often wrapped in special light-proof containers and stored in underground tombs and mausoleums, even today their colours can dazzle the eye and the scenes bring a long-dead civilization to life.

Although they were once plentiful in the Nile Valley, natural papyrus reed beds have long since disappeared from Egypt, and today the plant is cultivated in only a few places, specifically for the crafts and tourist-markets. There are a number of papyrus artists who are masters of their craft, and even factory-produced papyrus sheets are still painted by hand. These modern paintings are for the most part copies of antique papyrus pictures or of familiar scenes from wall paintings in temples, tombs and monuments, that depict significant events in ancient history. A similar-looking paper to papyrus is made for the cheaper end of the craft market from other raw materials such as banana leaf.

Weaving

The craft of carpet and rug weaving was introduced to Egypt during the Mamluk era; the carpet and rugs produced at this time featured geometric motifs and stylized representations of plants in vivid colours. Later, Ottoman influences introduced designs more typical of the refined Islamic style of Turkish carpets, where a greater and more subtle range of colours is used.

This is Egypt

The Egyptian weaving industry continued to thrive through the Ottoman period, but because it relied heavily on immigrant weavers to keep it going, the making of the traditional style of rugs and carpets, as depicted in many paintings by European artists, came to an end with the decline of Mamluk influence in the early 19th century.

In the 1950s, the flat weaving of woollen rugs and wall hangings was started as a development project by the artist and architect Ramses Wissa Wassef, who encouraged underprivileged children to take up weaving as an artistic outlet. Under his supervision they produced a naïve style of pictorial weaving in which bold colours are used in crude representations of animals, plants and rural scenes. The long-term result of this project has been a new creative era of handcrafted weavings, and the style first developed by the children has become a distinctive and modern Egyptian craft.

The Bedouins have a long tradition of weaving relatively crude rugs and utility items such as camel bags. The designs on these weavings tend to be simple geometric shapes that make use of the natural colours of different wools rather than dyed materials; however, Bedouin weavers do use brightly coloured cottons for decorating garments and textiles with lively embroidery.

Given the country's hot, dry desert climate, every town in Egypt supports a large number of vendors of fruit, sugar-cane and flower-based drinks. Carrying a trayful through Cairo's Khan-el-Khalili can mean negotiating a way through crowds of animals as well as humans.

Food and Drink

Egyptian cuisine is a wonderfully varied blend of traditional Middle Eastern fare, enriched by the influence of Turks, Greeks, Western Europeans, and neighbouring African and Arab states. It is based on homegrown foodstuffs, drawing heavily on seasonal and regional ingredients. Thropughout the country, food is sold in local markets, where the distinctive aroma of spices blends with the smell of fresh fruits and vegetables and huge baskets of flowers, and where incense burns to keep the flies away from trays of fresh dates and sweetmeats made of nuts and honey.

The main staple ingredients of Egyptian cooking are wheat, rice, pulses such as lentils, chickpeas and *fuul* or Egyptian beans, potatoes, salad vegetables and fruits, dairy produce, poultry, pigeon, lamb, and other meats, such as camel and goat. Grilled fish and seafood are favourite foods around the Mediterranean coast, in coastal Sinai, and in the Aswan region, which gets freshwater fish from Lake Nasser. In these different regions, sea bass, mullet, sea bream, tilapia, monkfish, giant prawns, squid, lobster and cuttlefish, are among the many varieties that can be found.

One of the great pleasures of eating in Egypt is the abundance of simple, wholesome and inexpensive food and drink available from street-side stalls and cafes. *Fuul* and *falafel* are the most widespread of these foods and have virtually become the

Cafés are not only a general centre of social life – some, such as Fishawi's in Khan-el-Khalili, have become well known as places for discussing literature, while others have a more political flavour or are centres for the law or other professions.

national dishes. *Fuul* beans can be cooked in a number of ways, but are commonly made into a partially mashed stew and flavoured with garlic and spices to make *fuul medames*, which is, like most Egyptian foods, spicy but not hot. *Falafel* is made of cooked, mashed and seasoned chickpeas or lava bean that are rolled into small patties before being deep-fried.

Fuul and *falafel* are served with salad and used as a filling for fresh Egyptian bread, a kind of pitta bread made from wheat flour and rolled out to produce a flat round bread, then split into an envelope shape and filled. Egyptians call bread *aish*, which means 'life', and it accompanies nearly every meal; it is common to use bread to pick up foods and dip into sauces, without using knives and forks.

Another speciality of Egyptian street fare is *kushari*, a bowl of noodles or macaroni topped with a very small amount of sauce. This can be quite deceiving to Western tastes, as the pasta on its own appears bland, but the sauce is packed with the punch of hot spices, onions and tomatoes and transforms the meal into a tasty, high-energy masterpiece.

Lamb is the most popular red meat (Muslims are forbidden to eat pork), and is used for classic Middle Eastern dishes: diced and grilled to make kebabs, minced to make meatballs called *kofta*, or roasted on revolving spits and carved into strips to make *shawarma*, eaten in envelopes of bread. Other favourite recipes are *shakshouka*, which is chopped lamb cooked with tomatoes and served with an egg, and *moza*, roasted lamb eaten with rice.

Although camel meat rarely appears on a restaurant menu, it is a relatively inexpensive meat that graces the tables of many a household. Rural people tend to know which day of the week their local butcher will have the type of meat that they want and plan their menus accordingly. Not much of any food is wasted in Egypt, and many dishes make use of liver and other offal.

Chicken is another staple ingredient, found usually in stews, roasted or grilled. Pigeons are reared in their thousands throughout the country and are brought live to markets, along with other poultry. Pigeon is not only a delicacy, but also has a place in ceremonies and festivals, particularly at Nubian weddings, where it is the custom for the bride and groom to be given pigeons as a token of prosperity and for them to feast on pigeons for many days afterwards.

Cooked vegetables, such as aubergines, cabbage, green beans, vine leaves and tomatoes, are nearly always fried before being used in sauces or soups, or in baked vegetarian dishes, such as *musaga*. Pickled vegetables, known as *makhallal*, are also very popular, and are often eaten with *tabouleh*, a mix of bulgur wheat, parsley, mint, tomatoes and onions.

Goats' and sheep's milk is mainly used to make yogurt and strong, salty cheeses. Milk is also an ingredient in desserts such as *mahallabiyah*, *om ali* and *kounafayeh*, where it is combined with cream, nuts, honey and spices. Honey is also the main flavouring in sticky pastries like *baqlawah*, which are sweet enough to satisfy even the strongest tooth. There is a great variety of fruits, including figs, dates, watermelons and pomegranates, and nuts are used in all forms of cookery.

Drinking tea and coffee is part of the way of life in Egypt: one of the country's most potent images is of men in flowing *galabiyyas*, sitting in street-side cafés and sipping at thick, sweet, dark aromatic coffee as they puff on their *sheeshas* (water-pipes) and watch the world go by. The bitter Bedouin version of coffee, known as *kahwah-al-hilo*, is made from coffee, cardamom and saffron. Tea, or *shai*, served hot, strong, black and sweet in a small glass, is drunk at any time of day. In some areas, particularly in Cairo, it is flavoured with fresh mint and called *shai na'ana*, but tea is rarely served with milk unless this is requested. Tea and coffee are almost always served with a lot of sugar, making them extremely sweet to most European palates.

Fruit-juice stalls are found everywhere in Egypt, selling glasses of freshly squeezed fruit juice or sweet, cloudy *asiir asab*, sugar cane juice. One typically Egyptian drink is bright-red *karkadeh*, an infusion of dried hibiscus flowers sweetened with sugar; although this can be drunk hot, it is more commonly served chilled, and it is one of the most refreshing ways to combat the effects of the sun.

The most widely encountered Egyptian beer, 'Stella', is a pale lager, and a few wines are made at the vineyards in the Nile Valley; the reds have evocative names like 'Nefertiti' and 'Omar Khayyam', while the better white wines for European palates include 'Gianaclis' and 'Patalomai'.

Fish markets specialize in the fresh produce of their region – those for seawater fish are found particularly around the coast of Sinai and along the northern Mediterranean coast, while freshwater fish are a delicacy in restaurants around Aswan.

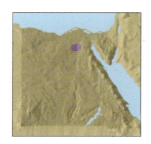

THE HUB OF THE NATION
GIZA, MEMPHIS AND CAIRO

Home to a sixth of Egypt's population, Cairo has long been the largest city in Africa. Its position at the north of the Nile, just south of the Delta region, gives it a commanding advantage over the country, well placed to reach the south by river and well provided for by the agricultural lands of the Delta.

At Giza, on the south-western edge of the capital's suburbs, the awe-inspiring Great Pyramids and the enigmatic Sphinx stand testament to the city's longevity and are perhaps the best-known symbols of Ancient Egypt; just to their south are the older and equally impressive pyramid complex at Saqqarah and the remains of Memphis, the capital city over 3,000 years ago.

A busy, bustling city, vibrant with the buzz of human activity, Cairo's heritage has been enriched with every passing age. Different peoples and religions have come and gone, each adding to the fabric of the city. Today, historic structures stand alongside modern buildings, recording this passage of time and reminding Caireans of the events and individuals that have made the country great.

At Tahrir Square in the city centre, the vast Egyptian Museum houses some of the most precious remnants of bygone ages. Here, many of the treasures and artworks that once adorned the tombs, temples and monuments of Pharaonic Egypt have now been housed, including the world-famous treasures discovered in the tomb of Tutankhamun.

Beyond the modern city centre, where gridlocked traffic vies for space with crowds of pedestrians, are the areas of Cairo where the architecture and atmosphere reflect the legacy of different religious and cultural periods. To the south of Tahrir Square is Old Cairo, in its day the centre of the city's activity, where the last remains of Fustat, the first Islamic seat of power, stand alongside the Ben Ezra Synagogue, one of the few remaining remnants of a once-flourishing Jewish community. The heart of Coptic Christianity, Old Cairo houses the Coptic Museum and has a number of churches dating back to an era when Christianity was predominant.

To the south-east, Islamic Cairo has many historic landmarks, including the magnificent mosques of Ibn Tulun and Sultan Hasan, and the Central Mosque built by Muhammad Ali, which dominates the skyline with its grand domes and elegant minarets. Begun as a fortress by Saladin in Crusader times, and further enriched at the end of the Mamluk era, the Citadel stands on a strategic hill overlooking the city. Around the Citadel are the Cities of the Dead, once-sacred mausoleums now inhabited by families of squatters. To the north, the Khan-al-Khalili is a myriad of bazaars, where every kind of craft is bought and sold, with an overpowering atmosphere that is a celebration of all things Egyptian.

THE HUB OF THE NATION

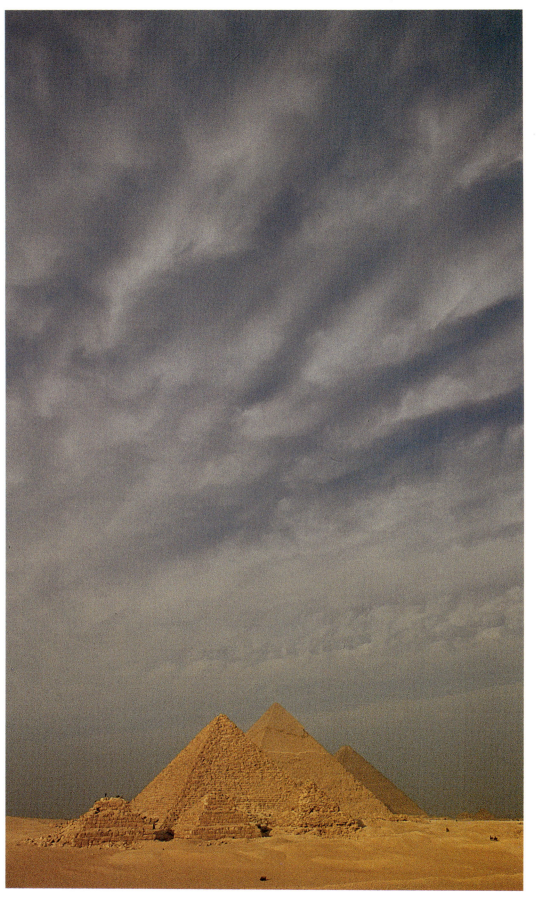

Cairo's best-known landmark, and the most recognizable symbol of the architectural achievements of the Ancient Egyptians, the complex of pyramids at what is now the suburb of Giza (left) *consists of three main pyramids, together with associated temples and tombs, and smaller pyramids, known as the Queen's Pyramids. Although many theories have been put forward, the actual engineering techniques and construction methods used to create the magnificent Pyramids of Menkaure (Mycerinus) and Khafre (Chephren) and the Great Pyramid of Khufu (Cheops), remain unsolved to this day. Standing alongside Khafre's Valley Temple like an ever-vigilant guardian of the complex, the mysterious Sphinx* (opposite, below) *was thought for years to have been carved in the image of Khafre or a deity. However, having observed water erosion on the Sphinx, a number of contemporary Egyptologists date it at 2,600 years older than Khafre's Pyramid. Just as the pharaohs chose this site as their eternal resting-place, so too the modern inhabitants of Cairo: the Muslim cemetery of Giza encroaches on the complex of funerary temples and pyramids* (opposite, above).

PREVIOUS PAGES
Page 36: *The architectural serenity of Cairo's ancient Islamic buildings provides its people with a quiet contrast to the bustling streets.*
Page 37: *Even in cramped urban conditions, the children of the capital are always full of vitality and interest in the city around them.*

The Pyramids of Giza

THE HUB OF THE NATION

In the tombs and funerary complexes of Giza, as throughout Ancient Egypt, masons used their skills to produce monumental artworks and architecture in stone. The deceased were represented by life-size statues, such as those in the temple of Qar (left). Many of these aesthetic masterpieces have, however, suffered from the disrespect of later generations: the Sphinx (below left) lost its nose to a Mamluk army's target practice, and its beard to the British Museum in London. The outer casing stones of the Great Pyramid of Khufu (Cheops) were removed and used in later buildings, thus revealing the internal construction of massive limestone blocks, each of which weighs between 2.5 and 15 tons (below).

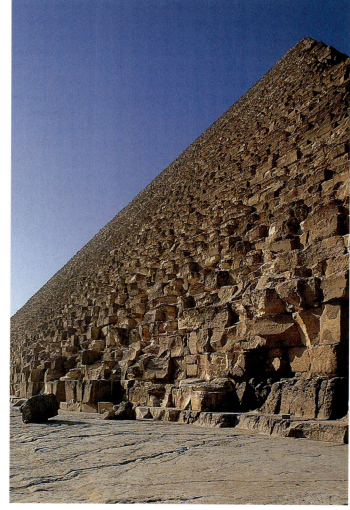

South of Giza, the ancient necropolis of Saqqarah is dominated by the funerary complex built for the 3rd-Dynasty King Zozer. The complex is surrounded by a high limestone wall with 14 detailed entrance gates carved into it; of these, 13 are false and only one a true entrance (below). In the centre of the complex, the Step Pyramid (right) is constructed from blocks of limestone, heralding a new departure from the earlier tradition of building mastabas (oblong tombs) from mud bricks. The Pyramid was originally covered with casing stones of white limestone, and at 62 metres (204 feet) high was the largest stone structure built at that time. This pioneering piece of architecture, designed by the first architect whose name has come down to us, Imhotep, is thought to be the forerunner of the great pyramids at Giza.

The tombs and temples around Saqqarah house exquisite examples of Ancient Egyptian art, which was used to depict every aspect of life and death, from life-size figures (top) to practical details of day-to-day activities. In the Mastaba of Ti, decorative reliefs show a range of agricultural scenes that give a remarkable insight to life in the 5th Dynasty – representations of hunting scenes in the marshes, harvesting the papyrus crops, ploughing and seeding in the fields, boatbuilding, craftsmen shaping pottery and fashioning gold jewellery and metalware, and servants feeding geese and cranes (left). This tomb art is invaluable in helping modern man understand the lifestyles and social interaction of the people that formed the society of Ancient Egypt (above).

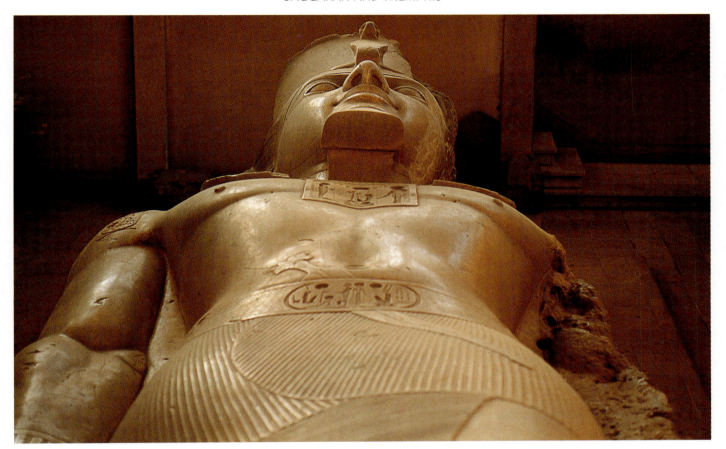

Saqqarah was used as a burial site throughout the Old Kingdom period (around 2613–2152 BC), serving the society that ruled from the nearby capital of Memphis. Although there is little left of Memphis today, a few impressive statues from different ages, such as the Colossus of Ramesses II (top) lie and stand in the Memphis Museum. The mastabas at Saqqarah were not confined to the burial of kings, but were also mausoleums for high-ranking officials; these too were ornate and decorated with sculptures, reliefs and paintings. The tomb of the 6th-Dynasty vizier Kagemni features fine reliefs depicting rural scenes (above), while that of his contemporary Mereruka boasts a life-size statue of that vizier emerging from a false doorway (right).

The Hub of the Nation

Living alongside the ancient past, the Cairo of today is a thriving modern city. Built on the sites of various settlements on this part of the Nile that date back to Paleolithic times, Greater Cairo encompasses the governorate of Giza, which stretches to the edge of the desert by the pyramids, several islands in the Nile itself, and the governorate of Cairo – a vast metropolis that sprawls out from the eastern bank of the river. Seen from the popular viewpoint of the 186-metre (614-feet) high modern Cairo Tower in the Gezira area, the bridges that link the districts make a picturesque contemporary cityscape when lit up at night (above).

More than just a watercourse running through the heart of the city, the Nile has a vast significance to the prosperity of the country, to the extent that its water levels had a direct relationship to the levels of taxation. The depth of the annual flooding traditionally determined the projected prosperity of the rural areas, so taxes were based on the potential yields from well-irrigated fields, and Nilometers were built as instruments for measuring the water of the river. The central octagonal column of the Roda Island Nilometer (left), built in 861, is marked off in gradations of about 54 centimetres (21 inches), and the surrounding walls carry scriptures from the Koran.

CAIRO: THE MODERN CAPITAL

Always busy, bustling and crowded, the streets of central Cairo (top) bear witness to the statistic that the city is home to nearly a sixth of the country's population, and is the largest city in the African continent. Yet, as in any great conurbation, children flock to playgrounds that are tucked away in unexpected corners (above). For less energetic recreation, vast billboards advertise the latest cinema productions from Egypt and abroad, which often depict subjects and lifestyles that are in stark contrast to the traditions of Muslim modesty (right).

THE HUB OF THE NATION

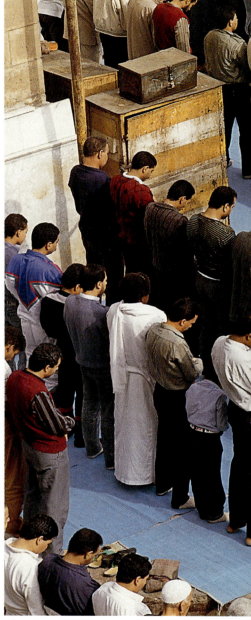

Although Egypt is predominantly a Muslim country, Cairo has a strong Christian heritage. In addition to the religious services, street decorations and celebrations commemorate the Coptic Christmas, which falls on 7 January each year (top left), following the old Julian calendar. For the devout, stalls selling Christian religious icons can be found in the backstreets of the Coptic quarter of Old Cairo (far left).

CAIRO'S PEOPLE

The people of Cairo form a society where much of everyday life takes place out in the open, on the streets. The Friday prayers are an important part in the lives of the Muslims who make up most of the population, and great crowds gather in Maydan al-Husayn (Hussein Square) to pray together (above). Even the essentials of life, like getting a morning shave, are performed as a visible part of street life (right).

In such a busy city, some find that the easiest way to weave quickly through the congestion of cars and other vehicles, animals, pedestrians and horse-drawn carts is by motorcycle (opposite, below near left). Other families escape the jammed thoroughfares and residential areas, and find a degree of peace and quiet by living on floating houseboats on the city's waterways (opposite, middle left).

The Hub of the Nation

The two greatest influences on the culture and contemporary history of Egypt have been the introduction of Islam and, in the 19th century, the country's independent infrastructure, instigated by Muhammad Ali. The magnificent Muhammad Ali Mosque (above) in the centre of Saladin's Citadel, dominating the skyline of Islamic Cairo to the south-east of the city centre, encompasses both of these influences. It was built between 1830 and 1848, at a time when Muhammad Ali overthrew the last of the Mamluks and set about the task of rebuilding Cairo into a modern city, bringing for the first time some semblance of order to the structure of the city planning; he also set about educating its population with the help of European scholars and scientists.

Completed in 1857, the Muhammad Ali Mosque is also known as the Alabaster Mosque, although the alabaster which originally lined the exterior, itself stripped from demolished Mamluk buildings, was in its turn taken by Muhammad Ali's successor, Abbas, to grace the walls of his own palace. Before prayers, devout Muslims wash their heads, faces, arms and feet in the holy waters of the eight-sided fountain in the centre of the forecourt (left).

Islamic Cairo and the City of the Dead

Islamic architecture features in every aspect of the city's buildings and structures, some of them unique to the capital. In the City of the Dead, or Northern Cemetery, which lies to the north-east of Islamic Cairo, the traditional domes, minarets and archways that are integral features of the exteriors of mosques throughout Egypt are mirrored in the design of the countless mausoleums (above), *making the area a miniature reflection of the greater city.*

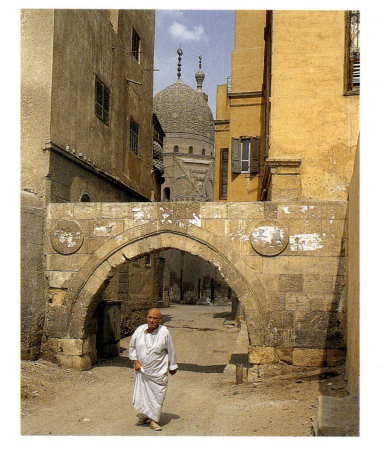

Due to chronic overcrowding in the city itself, these resting-places for the dead, many dating back to early Mamluk times in the 12th century, have also become homes for the living, and it is estimated that hundreds of thousands of Cairenes lead a squatter's life among the tombs. Houses have been built along the streets that bisect the cemeteries (right), *and even family plots are inhabited to provide a measure of shelter.*

THE HUB OF THE NATION

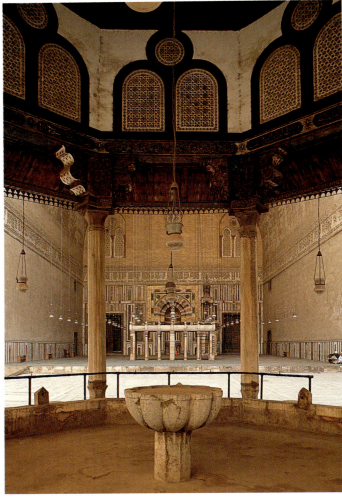

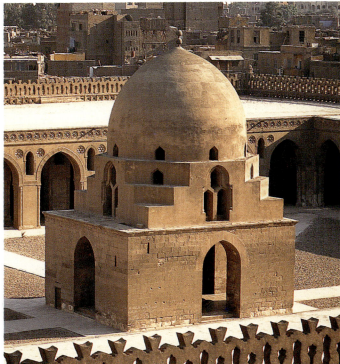

THE GREAT MOSQUES OF CAIRO

The architecture of the great mosques of Islamic Cairo draws its inspiration from throughout the Arab world. The oldest mosque in the city is that of Ibn Tulun (opposite, below right), which dates from the 9th century. A governor of Fustat under the rule of the Abbasids from Iraq who, at that time, were in control of the Muslim world, Ibn Tulun declared independence in 868 and founded his own dynasty. The mosque's unique minaret with a spiral staircase (opposite, above left) was probably influenced by the mosque at Samarra, from where the Abbasids originated.

First constructed in 1365, the Mosque of Sultan Hassan (opposite, above right) was later discovered to incorporate a series of major design faults. It was originally intended to have a minaret at each of its corners, but the plans had to be altered after one of them collapsed. A second minaret fell down some 260 years later, followed shortly by the dome. The mosque was reconstructed in 1671, and remains one of the largest mosques in the world. A haven of tranquillity amidst the teeming city, its massive scale is reinforced in the interior by the pendulous lights that hang from long chains (opposite, below left), a feature also used to great effect in the Mosque of al-Muayyad, constructed between 1415 and 1422 (right). One of the most ornate of Cairo's mosques, it makes use of the variant colours of different stones and derives its alternative name of the Red Mosque from the colour of its exterior.

GATES AND MERCHANTS' HOUSES

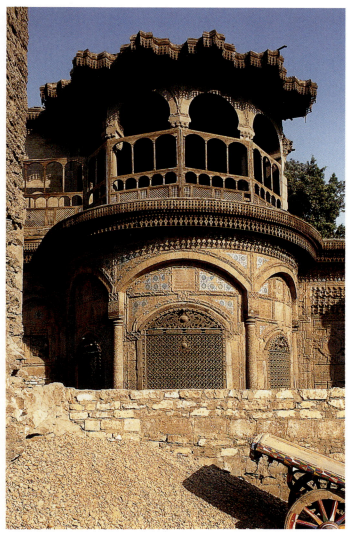

In Cairo, Islamic art in architecture is reflected in both private and public buildings. Formerly the house of a wealthy merchant of the 17th century, Bayt al-Sihaymi (opposite) *contains fine examples in its cool, elegant interior of the Islamic use of intricately carved wooden panels and lattice work. Another exquisite use of Islamic design in a private structure can be seen in the* Sabil-Kuttab, *or water fountain, of Ruqwuyyah Dudu* (above right), *built in 1761 by a lady from the Shahin Bay family.*

The minarets of the Mosque of al-Muayyad appear to have been placed to dominate the substantial fortified structure of the city's south gate, Bab Zuwaylah, built in 1092 (above). *A popular meeting place, with traders and passing traffic competing for space outside it, the gate is also an attractive subject for artists* (right).

53

The Hub of the Nation

In the heart of Islamic Cairo, the bazaar area of Khan-el-Khalili is constantly alive with the bustle of merchants and their customers. Its narrow streets are thronged with people heading for the many markets (above left), and the alleyways overflow with bustling workshops where craftsmen of all kinds still employ traditional skills handed down over generations. In Fishawi's and a myriad of other smoke-filled cafés, people gather to chat over endless glasses of sweet black tea and thick dark coffee throughout the day (left); but there are also calmer moments when traders can stand in their shop doorways and reflect on the day's business (above).

THE KHAN-EL-KHALILI

For Cairenes who live in the old Islamic city, much of their everyday shopping is done in the markets around Khan-el-Khalili, where they buy spices and groceries from shops that display their goods by the sackload (top). Perfume stalls advertise their wares with an array of bottles containing a baffling variety of flower essences and complex scents that have been produced locally since ancient times (right). Modernity is never far away, however, and even the most traditional of pastimes, the sheesha (water-pipe), is likely to be accompanied by reminders of the technological age (above).

THE HUB OF THE NATION

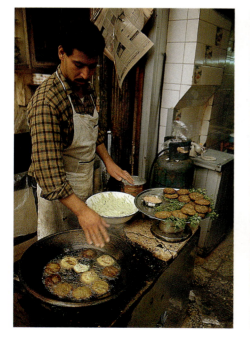

Fresh produce to supply both the kitchens of Cairo homes and the myriad side-street stalls, is abundant in the food markets of Khan-el-Khalili, where vendors offer a wide range of foodstuffs to eat on the spot or to take away. Here, cartons of fish tower above a trader and his stall (above); a favourite open-air fast snack is falafel, *patties of ground pulses dropped into hot oil and fried until crisp (far left); and for the sweet-toothed, there is always someone close at hand selling trays of honey-soaked, nutty* baqlawah, *the local sweetmeat (left).*

In Cairo, the combination of a hot climate and very limited access to refrigeration — and even less in smaller cities and towns — means that meat sold in the markets has been freshly butchered the same day (above). Many popular Egyptian dishes involve pigeons and doves, and these are commercially reared and, along with chickens and ducks, brought live to the markets (right), to be bought and sold as fresh as possible.

The Hub of the Nation

Every corner of the streets and alleyways of Cairo buzzes with life and vibrancy: in secluded courtyards, blacksmiths heat and forge their ironware (top); surrounded by colourful appliquéd cotton cloths, the tent-makers sew together panels for ceremonial marquees (left); on their way from market, women stop to make conversation in the middle of the street (above); a flock of sheep seek out a shady doorway to hide from the intense heat of the midday sun (opposite, above left); a family sits outside on a street corner, just watching the world go by (opposite, above right); dwarfed by the giant, fortress-like architecture of the old city gate of Bab Zuwaylah, a young boy makes his way home bearing food from a local street stall (opposite, below).

KHAN-EL-KHALILI: CRAFTS AND STREET LIFE

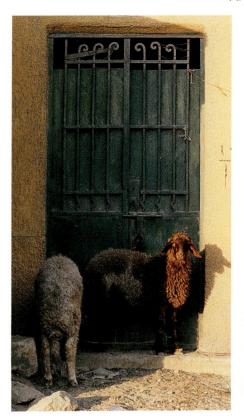

THE NILE DELTA

NORTH TO ALEXANDRIA AND THE COAST

North of Cairo, the Nile begins to fan out and disperse its waters over a massive area to produce the rich farmlands of the Nile Delta. This area provides the capital with the majority of its food as well as producing the valuable cotton cash crop for export and the home textile industry. The agricultural plains finally run out at the northern, Mediterranean coast, covering an area between the cities of Alexandria to the west and Port Said to the east.

Outside the cities, life in the rural regions continues to revolve around the natural cycles of the land. Long festivals, known as *moulids*, are held to mark saints' birthdays and such events as the cotton harvest. These are colourful and exciting celebrations, when otherwise tranquil lives, bound to the timeless rhythms of the land, are transformed with the vibrancy of song, dance and religious devotion.

At the northern end of the Suez Canal, Port Said not only thrives on trade as a free port, but also benefits from the recreational atmosphere of uncluttered Mediterranean beaches. It is a prime holiday destination for many Egyptians, but as yet has attracted comparatively few foreign visitors. Along the coast to the west, the lakes and marshes of the Delta form much-needed wetlands in a country that is largely engulfed by desert sands.

West of Lake Burullus stands the town of Rosetta, whose name remains famous thanks to the Rosetta Stone, which was discovered in 1799. Study of the engravings on the Stone enabled 19th-century scholars to decipher hieroglyphs for the first time, thus providing a vital key to Pharaonic history. The architecture of the Delta is quite distinct from that in other parts of Egypt, and fine examples of the Ottoman style can still be seen in Rosetta and neighbouring Fuwah.

Built on a grand scale, modern Alexandria has been influenced as much by European colonialism as by its underlying Greco-Roman and Ancient Egyptian history. A few relics of these earlier ages still grace the city, and archaeological investigation continues into the site of the former lighthouse, one of the Seven Wonders of the Ancient world. Before the 1960s Alexandria was renowned for its liberal atmosphere and was a magnet for avant-garde artistic endeavours, and it remains a cosmopolitan melting pot of peoples and styles.

To the south and west of the green haven of the Delta, the deserts are barren and unforgiving – so much so that when the early Christians sought a hermitage they chose the desert at Wadi al-Natrun, far enough from civilization for an ecclesiastical retreat, yet close enough to the Delta to supply their wells with water. The monasteries they built over 1,000 years ago are still inhabited, and the Coptic Pope is chosen from the monks of al-Natrun.

THE NILE DELTA

In the Nile Delta to the north of Cairo, the life of the agricultural community revolves around the cycles of nature as it has done since prehistoric times. The waters of the river irrigate the land and provide a natural fishing-ground for the fishermen of Fuwah (above). Others work the dry land around, and the wool trade gives a traditional living to many a family (left).

PREVIOUS PAGES
Page 60: Sunset over the Old Arab Quarter, Alexandria.
Page 61: *A monk reads the Bible in the Deir Anba Bishoy at Wadi al-Natrun.*

Traditional Life in the Nile Delta

Modern technology has had relatively little impact on the rural community of the Delta, and only the occasional ageing American car can be seen on the country roads where once animal power alone held sway (above). In a region where the old hand-farming practices are still predominant, age-old methods of preparing wool thread for the textile industry from raw fleeces continue to be employed (right).

THE NILE DELTA

Occasional festivals interrupt the changeless rhythm of the seasons and transform the normally quiet Delta towns into bustling, colourful scenes. These moulids *are celebratory events held to mark specific landmarks in the year, such as harvests or religious anniversaries. Combining both reasons, one of the biggest festivals, the* Moulid of Sayyid Ahmad al-Badawi, *an influential Sufi Muslim of the 13th century, marks the end of the cotton harvest each October. In the Central Delta region, thousands of people flock from neighbouring villages to* Tanta (left), *Egypt's fifth-largest city and al-Badawi's resting-place, to join in the celebrations* (below left).

Like other towns where festivals take place, the usually sedate provincial city comes to life during the time of the moulid, *with brightly coloured awnings appearing on street corners* (below), *adding to the party atmosphere.*

TANTA: THE OCTOBER *MOULID*

For street traders and shopkeepers, the *moulids* are the busiest time of the year, and shop fronts in Tanta stay illuminated until late in the evening (top), hoping for a last customer. But shopping is not the only attraction for the crowds of festival-goers: travelling fairgrounds are welcomed into the city, offering all the traditional games and rides (right), and sideshow artists such as 'Captain Costa's Daredevil Act' (above) come from all over the Mediterranean region to perform death-defying feats of showmanship.

THE NILE DELTA

On the eastern Mediterranean coast, the 19th-century city of Port Said stands at the mouth of the Suez Canal, one of the busiest shipping routes in the world, linking Europe with the Indian Ocean and beyond, and providing a valuable trade route between East and West. In the city itself, trade has been built up largely by its status as a duty-free port that has attracted traders – and a fair share of smugglers – in its time, particularly around the bustling harbour (above). Trade with the crews and passengers of the cruise ships that dock here (left) continues to provide the city with valuable income.

West of Port Said and set back inland along the mouth of the eastern branch of the Nile, Damietta is the provincial capital. It was once a thriving port city, trading mainly in agricultural produce and textiles, but much of this trade has now gone to neighbouring Port Said. Possibly because of this ostensible decline, Damietta has managed to retain a more traditional, older lifestyle, with an atmosphere more like that of a provincial town than a bustling city. In a place where there is always time to sit and read verses from the Koran (above), the pace of life is gentle and the transport for people, goods or even piles of gilded chairs is by muscle, not motor, power (right).

The Nile Delta

Quite different from the architectural designs used elsewhere in Egypt, Delta-style mansion houses are constructed using coloured brickwork, with the pointing often picked out in contrasting colours of paint. One of the finest examples of this form of decoration is the Galal House in Rosetta (above); the Ottomans also built similar houses in Damietta and many other Delta towns.

For visitors who decide to make the one-hour journey to Rosetta from Alexandria, travelling in a characterful old Buick or Dodge car pressed into service as a taxi can make for a memorable ride (left).

THE STREETS OF ROSETTA

The name of Rosetta became internationally famous through the discovery in 1799 of a carved stone that held inscriptions in both Greek and hieroglyphics; the Rosetta Stone provided the first, vital key to translating all the scriptures of Ancient Egypt. However, other than establishing the town's name, this find had little effect on the ways of its residents; some live a laid-back life, propped up against the Delta-style mansions (above right), which stand alongside more wide-spread arabesque designs in the shade of date palms (right).

HISTORIC AND MODERN ALEXANDRIA

West of Rosetta, the port of Alexandria is Egypt's second city. Situated on the Mediterranean coast at the edge of the Delta where the green lands meet the desert, it is a cosmopolitan city that has grown through its colonial days to mirror many of the cities on the European side of the Mediterranean. The greater part of its city centre architecture is based on 19th- and 20th-century European designs, with grand buildings and an impressive Corniche that flanks the sea round a semicircular bay (above). Despite this classical backdrop, the modern city still has a typically Egyptian atmosphere (right); the fishing fleet takes advantage of the sea to bring in the day's catch to be sold in the markets (below right).

Beyond the centre the city spreads out to encompass far older parts. The Old Arab Quarter faces onto the seafront along the western end of Alexandria and stretches past the fishing port to the promontary where the Pharos, the ancient lighthouse that was one of the Seven Wonders of the Ancient world, once stood. Today all that remains of the lighthouse are lively carvings found in the sea nearby (opposite, below left), while the site itself is occupied by Fort Qayt Bay (opposite, above) constructed during the 1480s and subsequently further fortified by Muhammad Ali. It is one of Alexandria's most famous and visited landmarks, rivalling other such historic sights as the Roman Theatre (opposite, below right), dating back to the 2nd century.

The Nile Delta

With its coastal links to Europe, Alexandria was the brainchild of Alexander the Great, who founded a capital city here away from the Nile in the 4th century BC. Since Alexander's time the city has seen empires rise and fall, and rebellions and uprisings have been played out on its historic streets. It has been the home of great scholars such as the mathematician Euclid, a seat of learning and a store of knowledge, the site of one of the earliest and greatest libraries of the Ancient world. Alexandria was the capital of historical and romantic figures such as Cleopatra, with her exploits and intrigues with and against the Romans, and, centuries later, was a renaissance city for Muhammad Ali. In the years after World War II, the city managed to be both a colonial stronghold and a hotbed of fervent nationalism.

EVERYDAY LIFE IN ALEXANDRIA

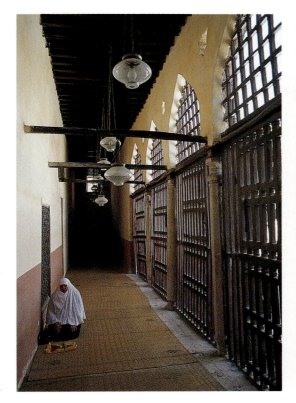

Despite Alexandria's extraordinary history, for most of its population of 4,000,000 the city is simply their home where their daily lives continue, oblivious for the greater part to the cosmopolitan past. Fishermen launch their boats from the city's beaches (opposite, top), and shopkeepers and traders sell everything from imported Brazilian coffee in European-style cafés (opposite, middle left) to locally produced paper bags (opposite, bottom). From a cosy police box (opposite, middle right) two policemen keep watch over streets where workers going about their daily business pass in front of small mosques (above right). In the north of the city near Anfushi Bay, the Mosque of al-Tabarna offers the opportunity to escape from the bustle of the streets and spend time in prayer (above); another, somewhat less devout, form of relaxation is found on the beaches of the Mediterranean, where Alexandrian families maintain a certain modesty and formality while soaking up the sun (below right); the European influence extends to clothing, and most men wear Western styles.

THE NILE DELTA

South of Alexandria, just beyond the irrigated fields of the Delta, the parched desert takes a hold of the country. It was in this direction that the early Egyptian Christians fled, in the face of relentless persecution by the then pagan society of Alexandria. The power of the Copts has ebbed and flowed since the early beginnings – Christianity became the state religion in the 4th century, but was later superseded in this role by Islam, and today Coptic Christians make up just under a tenth of the population of the country. At Wadi al-Natrun in a dried river valley they found fertile soil, but the water of the springs and lakes turned out to be brackish. Not in the least deterred by these unpromising conditions, they built monasteries and churches here and started what has remained a stronghold of Coptic Christianity ever since.

The largest of the four monastery complexes at Wadi al-Natrun is Deir Anba Bishoy (below left), where some 200 monks pass lives of contemplation and worship in buildings that have been destroyed and restored on more than one occasion in their turbulent history (opposite, below).

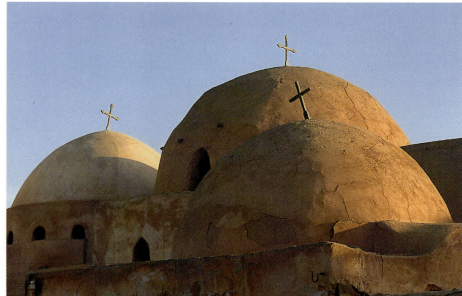

Within each monastery complex stand a number of churches and chapels, often characterized by rounded roofs (above right): the main church in the Bishoy complex is the 9th-century Church of St Bishoy (opposite, above left), where the latest restoration was completed in 1957. The nearby Deir al-Suryan is a Syrian monastery whose principal church, the Church of the Virgin, contains an evocative Madonna and Child (opposite, below right); this complex was built just 500 metres from St Bishoy following a bitter theological dispute in the 6th century.

The most remote and isolated of the four monasteries, Deir Anba Baramus, is also known as the Roman Monastery, having been founded by Maximus and Domidus, sons of the Roman Emperor Valentinus. As in other monasteries, its old press and working tools have been preserved (above). Further south along the wadi stands the fourth and oldest monastery, Deir Abu Maqar, which is said to have been founded by St Macarius in the 4th century.

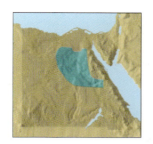

Along the Nile to the Valley of the Kings
South to Luxor

South-east along the Nile from Wadi al-Natrun, the Fayyum area is a lily pad of green on the edge of a lake in the desert, fed by a system of canals that have brought the waters of the Nile to a natural depression in the land. One of man's earliest irrigation projects, the canals date back to ancient times, and even today huge water wheels groan and creak as they heave the water along its course. The people of the Fayyum region are mainly farmers, although some make a living from fishing in the great lake, known as Birket Qarun. On the edge of the desert, where Bedouin tribes continue to maintain their traditional semi-nomadic life, the 12th-Dynasty temples at Medinet Ma'adi and the Collapsed Pyramid at Maydum make it clear that this area was once an important cultural centre in Pharaonic Egypt.

South of the Fayyum, the Nile forms the core of Middle Egypt, the site both of ancient monuments and the later Red and White Monasteries at Sohag; these were begun in the 5th century and are among the oldest surviving Christian buildings. The southern end of this stretch of water leads to Upper Egypt, the main seat of power for generations of Pharaonic kings. The temples, monuments and tombs that have withstood the ravages of time here are more numerous and more magnificent than in any other part of the country. The religious centres at Abydos and Dendarah, which were developed by the New Kingdom pharaohs and later by the Greco-Romans, were the base for the aesthetic and creative arts that adorned the monumental structures. The particular blend of art and architecture found here was established on ancient techniques to portray ancient beliefs, yet through succeeding eras it has been an inspiration to new developments, each one a marvel of its own time.

The villagers who live along this part of the Nile Valley, and the townsfolk of Luxor and New Qurnah on the West Bank, live in the shadow of a rich history, where the ancient is a part of modern life, with the Temple of Luxor in the very centre of the town and Karnak on its outskirts. On the West Bank of the river at Luxor, sheep graze at the feet of the Colossi of Memnon, gigantic monolithic sculptures that have weathered into surreal guardians of the land, gatemen to the complex of tombs and temples that lies behind them.

In the Valley of the Kings and the Valley of the Queens beyond, the desert sands have preserved over the centuries the hidden burial sites of royalty, nobles and the workmen who constructed them. The tombs that have been rediscovered have surprised the world with their riches; in particular, the still exquisite and richly colourful tomb paintings, such as those in the Tomb of Nefertari, give invaluable clues to the lives and times of their occupants.

ALONG THE NILE TO THE VALLEY OF THE KINGS

Branching away from the Nile, a system of canals transports water to the desert areas, bringing agriculture and life to the Fayyum, a region of small settlements of farming communities and fishing families along the edge of Birket Qarun. In the fields outside Madinat al-Fayyum, or Fayyum City, the centre of this tranquil agricultural area, shepherds tend their sheep as did their ancestors in centuries past (above), *and the bright clothes of the young women and children bring a splash of colour to their surroundings* (left).

PREVIOUS PAGES
Page 76: *Seated colossi of Ramesses II flank the entrance to the Second Court at the Luxor Temple.*
Page 77: *Fellaheen in the lush agricultural land of the Nile Valley.*

A typical sight throughout the Fayyum area, giant water wheels (above) have been used for millennia to maintain the flow in the irrigation canals by lifting the water to higher channels, from where it is dispersed by gravity.

The agricultural land in this region is among the most productive in Egypt. Although it continues to be farmed in small family plots, using human, rather than mechanized, labour, the cumulative yield of such vital crops as cotton helps to boost the country's production of raw materials. The great bales of straw, like other agricultural produce from the area, are taken on the first leg of their journey from Fayyum by the traditional form of transport, donkey and cart (right).

The Fayyum area has been a home for human settlements since Neolithic times, and through the ages very different societies have been attracted to its fertile lands. On the north-eastern edge of the Fayyum, where the cultivated areas meet the desert, stands a pyramid complex that is believed to have been built 4,600 years ago. The construction of the Maydum Pyramid (above) is attributed either to Huni, the last ruler of the 3rd Dynasty, or to his son Sneferu, the first king of the 4th Dynasty. Because its outer casing is now lost, it is also referred to as the Collapsed Pyramid of Maydum. The pyramid may represent a transitional stage in the development from the stepped pyramid form, such as that of Zozer, to the true pyramids at Giza – the surviving stepped pyramid core may have been experimentally clad to create a true pyramid shape that failed to withstand the ravages of time and climate. On the opposite, western side of the Fayyum, still partly enveloped by the sands, stand the ruins of an ancient town and temple complex, Madinat al-Maadi (right). Built between 1844 and 1787 BC for the 12th-Dynasty pharaohs Amenemhat III and Amenemhat IV, the temple was used for worship during later periods, and the site was even extended in the Ptolemaic period of 404–330 BC.

Among the agricultural crops of the Fayyum are a number of flowers that are grown nowhere else in Egypt. The spectacular displays of fields full of camomile flowers are harvested (opposite) for use in herbal teas and for flavourings.

Ancient Monuments of Middle Egypt

South along the Nile from Fayyum into Middle Egypt, the 39 impressive rock-cut tombs at Bani Hasan date from the 11th and 12th Dynasties of the Middle Kingdom. The extensive murals and architectural styles inside (left) give an invaluable insight into the society that lived in this area during the period 2040–1783 BC, a time when many cult gods, such as Thoth, the moon god and divine scribe, were worshipped. Thoth was sometimes represented as a great white baboon, and across the Nile, on the West Bank, mummified baboons have been found at Tunah al-Gabal (top). The colossal statues of baboons at Al-Ashmunayn (above) date from the 13th Dynasty, and a temple to Thoth was built there on the site of an earlier one as late as the 4th century BC (opposite).

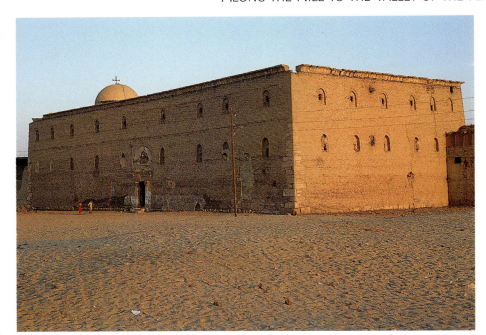
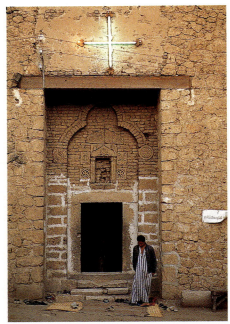

Further south along the Nile in Middle Egypt, the area around Sohag became a stronghold of Christianity in the 5th century, and just outside the modern-day town stand the two monasteries founded during that time. The larger of the pair is Deir al-Abyad or the White Monastery (opposite), so-called from the dazzling white limestone used in its construction. It is also known as Deir Anba Shenudah or the Monastery of St Shenute, paying homage to its foundation in 440 by a monk of that name, who was later canonized. The Church of St Shenute (left) and the monastery are still used for worship by a small community of monks, and there is a Coptic school in the old complex (above).

The smaller monastery (top left), founded by Besa, a follower of Shenute, also has two names: Deir al-Ahmar or the Red Monastery, reflecting its construction of red bricks, and Deir Anba Bishoy or the Monastery of St Bishoi. Since their foundation, both monasteries have been attacked and even sacked, and have also undergone a series of restorations; the structures that remain today, with their visible repairs (top right) represent a collage of styles that chronicle the development of Coptic architecture.

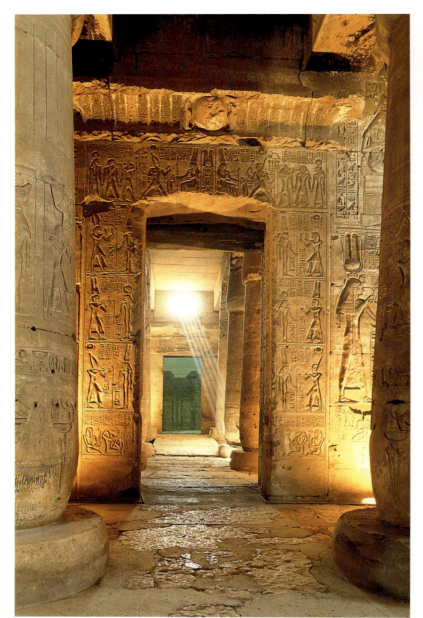
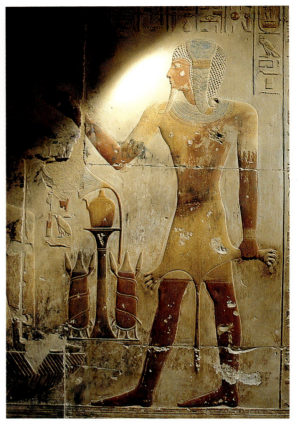

South-east of Sohag along the Nile, the holy city of Abydos was one of the most important cult centres of the Ancient Egyptians, who worshipped the god Osiris. Even before the Osiris cult became popular, the area was used as a prehistoric necropolis; mythology held that the entrance to the Underworld was in a gap in the mountains just behind the site. The link with Osiris may tie in with the earliest god recorded at Abydos – Khent-Amenty, a god of the dead who took the form of a dog – because other, later dog-like gods, such as Anubis, the overseer of enbalming, and Wepwawet, the messenger of kings, were associated with Osiris. Legends apart, it is generally agreed that Osiris was installed as lord of Abydos during the Old Kingdom era, and that the site took on its important role in the 2nd Dynasty, when the capital was at Memphis.

UPPER EGYPT: TEMPLES OF ABYDOS AND DENDARAH

Of the temples that still stand at Abydos, the most magnificent is the Temple of Seti I (opposite, top left and top right), which dates from 1306–1290 BC. Most of the arts used in the decoration of the Abydos temples come from this time; it was an era of artistic renaissance, when the craftsmen of the New Kingdom refined and perfected the styles, such as high-relief murals (opposite, middle left), that had been handed down from the Old Kingdom.

Evidence of the practice of drawing on earlier themes for latter-day temples can be found further south along the river at Dendarah. Shrines to Hathor, the ancient goddess of love and worldly pleasures, had existed here since pre-Dynastic times, but the magnificent Temple of Hathor that stands on the site today was built during the later Ptolemaic and Greco-Roman eras, between about 125 BC and AD 50, when it was left unfinished. The façade (opposite, bottom) combines Corinthian capitals with carved heads of Hathor; these heads, which hark back to much earlier decorative styles of architecture, are also used on the columns in the Hypostyle Hall (right) and on the Chapel of the New Year (above), where offerings to the goddess were made.

ALONG THE NILE TO THE VALLEY OF THE KINGS

Built on the East Bank of the Nile, with temples in its centre, Luxor is the closest major town to the Ancient Egyptian capital of Thebes and to the Valley of the Kings, just across the river. Its situation has made it one of the prime destinations for tourists, and most of its income derives from foreign visitors. Despite this influx of potential outside influences, Luxor has not become characterless or bland, and retains an unspoilt, typically Egyptian feel.

Town Life in Luxor

As the evening sun sets over the Nile, graceful *felluccas can be seen sailing quietly to their Luxor moorings in a timeless scene (opposite, above). In the town itself, the Egyptian pastimes of smoking* sheeshas, *drinking coffee and playing backgammon in street-side cafés (opposite, below) have been thankfully left unchallenged by the ubiquitous modern, international fast-food outlets that are found in the world's other major tourist areas. Here, the drivers of horse-drawn* calèshes *wait patiently for the trade they know will arrive eventually (right), and the townsfolk are content to take time off and to sit and watch the world go by from their balconies (above).*

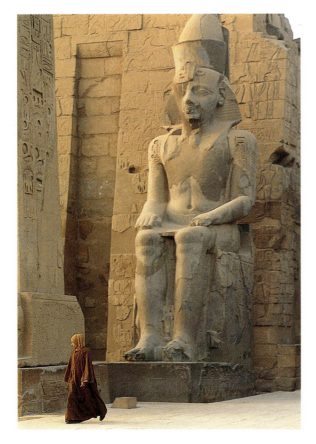

Alongside the waterfront promenade in the very heart of Luxor, the Luxor Temple was founded in the 14th century BC by the 18th-Dynasty king Amenophis III, and was dedicated to the Theban Triad of gods, Amun, Mut and Khonsu. However, around this time Amun was supplanted in popularity among many people by the sun-god Aten. Amenophis's son assumed the name Akhenaten in honour of the god, stopped work on the Luxor Temple, erased the symbols of his father and built a shrine to Aten by the side of the Temple. After Akhenaten's death, building work was started again by Tutankhamun and Horemheb, who had their own reliefs added to the court. Ramesses II left his mark on the Temple by adding another colonnaded court and a pylon for an entrance gate, and having six colossal statues of himself placed in front of the entrance, flanked by two great obelisks. Two of the enthroned colossi still remain (left), but only one of the obelisks survives in its original place – the other was removed to Paris in the 19th century. Nearly a thousand years after the Temple's foundation, an avenue of Sphinxes flanking a path to the Karnak Temple (above) was erected at the behest of Nectanebo I in the 4th century BC.

The monumental architecture at the Luxor Temple is a marvellous demonstration of how refined art was incorporated into the design of buildings in the New Kingdom era. The columns used for the colonnaded courts were carved to represent giant papyrus stems (opposite, below), and the great attention to detail is illustrated by the serpent-headed crown carved on the colossal head of Ramesses II (opposite, above left). The same crown is seen on an earlier representation of Tuthmosis III (opposite, above right) – a painted high relief, found in his temple dedicated to the god Amun on the West Bank, and now in the Luxor Museum of Ancient Egyptian Art.

Ancient Karnak

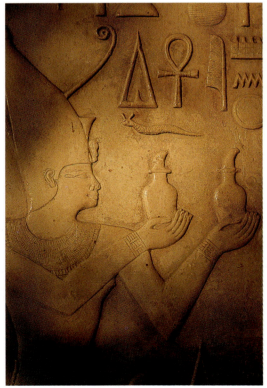

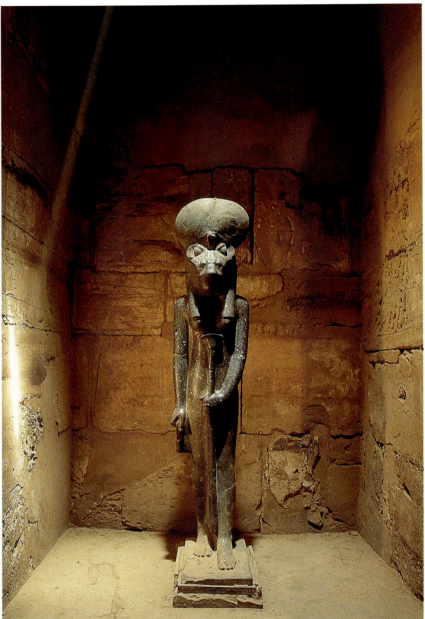

On the northern outskirts of Luxor, the Karnak Temple is a massive complex of temples, with courtyards and halls, obelisks, colossi, massive pylons and even a sacred lake, all within a walled area and known collectively as the Precinct of Amun. Over a period of about 1,300 years, it was added to and altered by successive generations who left hieroglyphs, artworks and statues (above left). Among these, many scenes of devotional offering (left) have helped later generations to understand the religious practices of Ancient Egypt. The ruins of the Temple of Ptah, originally constructed by Tuthmosis III, are against the north wall of the Precinct; hidden within the south chapel is a statue of Sekhmet in the form of a lion (above).

Perhaps the most impressive feature of the complex, and one that has a humbling effect on anyone who enters it, the massive Hypostyle Hall in the centre of the Temple of Amun (opposite) stands on an area of 6,000 square metres (9,300 square feet). It was built using 134 columns – the 12 which line the processional way down the centre were erected by Seti I, and Ramesses II added 122 columns behind them.

The waters of the Nile have always provided the principal lifeline through the surrounding deserts of Egypt; they have made it possible for agriculture to flourish, and have enabled generation after generation to establish communities along its banks. On the floodplains near Luxor, as throughout the Nile Valley, the fellaheen who work the fields (above) are locked in a timeless empathy with the land. Here, even the ubiquitous cafés are outdoor ones (left), reflecting the importance and traditions of the land.

LIFE AROUND THE UPPER NILE

The fellaheen of the Nile Valley lead uncomplicated lives, for the most part without many of the trappings of Western societies. Inside a typical, simple dwelling (above right), the sparse furnishings and traditional vibrant blue of the walls are enlivened by Koranic hangings and pages torn from magazines.

With the villages of the West Bank cut off by the river from Luxor town on the East bank, crossing the Nile plays a major part in the everyday lives of most people in the area. A trio of ferries runs back and forth all day, connecting the two halves of the greater community (right), while special, and more expensive, ferries cater for the vast numbers of visitors to this historic part of the country.

THE WEST BANK TEMPLES

The West Bank, the foothills of the old capital of Thebes across the Nile from Luxor, is one of the world's richest areas of architectural monuments, where the stupendous temples and tombs left by an ancient civilization have made the names of the New Kingdom rulers truly immortal. Dating from the mid-15th century BC, the Mortuary Temple of the 18th-Dynasty Queen Hatshepsut (top) is a magnificent construction of colonnades and terraces, incorporating sanctuaries and chapels dedicated to the gods, among them the Chapel of Hathor (right). The Colossi of Memnon (above), representing Amenophis III, were carved about a century later. Several monumental pieces relating to Ramesses II, who ruled in the 13th century BC, survive to this day. Though plundered and left as ruins, his mortuary temple, known as the Ramesseum (opposite), is still a dramatic sight. A further century later, Ramesses III enclosed his mortuary temple, Madinat Habu, in a massive complex of temples and chapels, and decorated it with reliefs, some based on those in the Ramesseum (above right).

The everyday fact that the sun sets in the west inspired the Ancient Egyptians to look to the west as a burial ground in what might be a gateway to the afterlife. To this end, the entire area of Thebes was devoted to tombs and temples – not only for royalty, but also for courtiers and nobles and even the workmen themselves, the artisans who created the masterpieces in the royal tombs during the 19th and 20th Dynasties. Many tomb paintings in the Valley of the Kings are based around this concept of preparing for the afterlife, and the artisans went to a great deal of trouble to make sure that their own tombs also contained symbolic reliefs that described the passage of the deceased from this life to the next.

In the tomb of Anherke, the chief workman, Anubis, the jackal-headed god who was the overseer of embalming, is portrayed in the complex process of preparing the artisan's mummy for the afterlife (left) and leading the deceased to Osiris, the god of the underworld and, perhaps surprisingly, fertility (below left). As well as the more macabre aspects of the afterworld, the reliefs incorporate elements of Egyptian life, for example the harpist (below), which help modern-day Egyptologists to establish the exact form of everyday objects such as musical instruments.

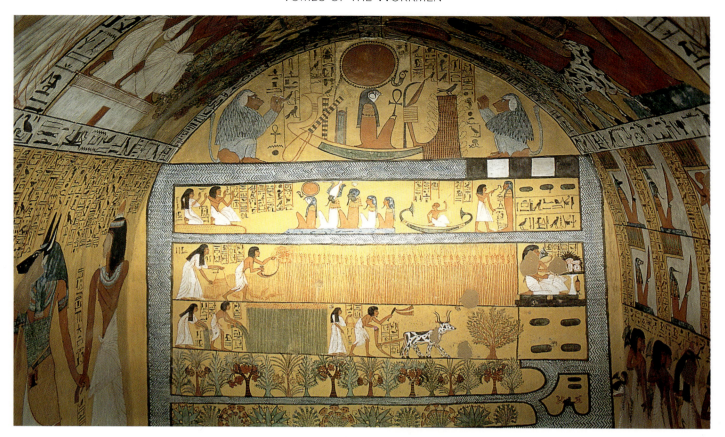

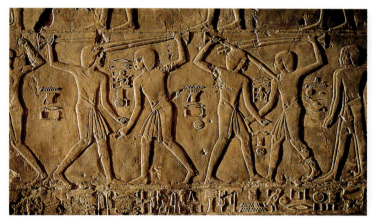

Set in the hills to the north of the Madinat Habu complex, many of the tombs around the Workmen's Village are comprised of only a single chamber; however, the rich, vivid colours of their wall paintings are among the finest that can be seen by the public. The Tomb of Sennedjem (top), a serving man in the Place of Truth, as the village was known, features scenes of the 'fields of the Afterlife' and the deceased's passage there, accompanied by the god Anubis.

Near the Mortuary Temple of Hapshetsut, just south of the Valley of the Kings, the relief carvings in the 18th-Dynasty Asasif Tombs include the themes of daily life and relaxation. The reliefs in the Tomb of the steward Kheru-ef (above and right) use every available inch of space above, below and between the lively figures to convey information.

TOMBS OF THE ROYALS AND NOBLES

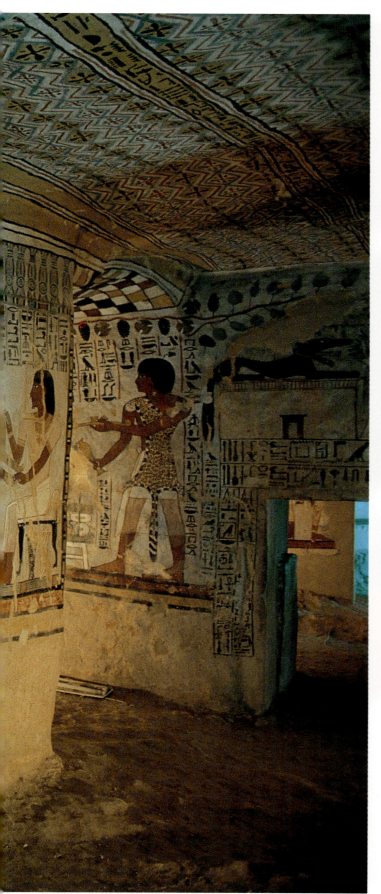

The Tombs of the Nobles and Queens have a different decorative content to those of the workmen: in addition to the ubiquitous funerary and afterlife scenes, such as the professional mourners depicted in the Tomb of Ramose (above), *the murals often show the deceased's areas of responsibility and their court and political lives. Often referred to as the Tomb of Vines, the Tomb of Sennufer* (left) *includes grapes and vines, illustrating that Sennufer was responsible for local viticulture, in addition to being mayor of Thebes. Murals in the tomb of the overseer Rekhmire show the state-craftsmen at work* (above middle), *and a relief from the Valley of the Queens pictures royal figures engaged in court duties* (top).

Along the Nile to the Valley of the Kings

Even among the ruined temples and tombs of Thebes, a prime destination for tourists, the rural life of Egyptian villagers continues in its old ways. The old village of Qurnah (left), nestling in the very heart of the necropolis, is thought to have grown up as a village community that made its living from robbing tombs. The practice has continued for centuries, and the full extent of the undiscovered treasures from the area is still a subject of speculation by Egyptologists and tomb robbers alike, since access to the extensive site is largely uncontrolled, especially beyond the known excavations. The donkey tracks that meander up the mountain sides from Qurnah to the Valley of the Kings (opposite, below) are used as footpaths by the locals.

Village Life on the West Bank

In an effort to relocate the village of Qurnah from among the ruins of Thebes, the acclaimed architect Hassan Fathy was commissioned to create a model village nearby; he used traditional methods of mud-brick construction that harked back to the surviving buildings of the Ancient Egyptians. However, on its completion in 1948, New Qurnah was not immediately popular, and the locals, not wanting to shift to a farming-based economy, flooded it in protest. Although the old village has never been abandoned, the new one eventually became occupied. Today, New Qurnah is a thriving agricultural village, with a bustling produce market (opposite, above left) *and a flourishing livestock industry in front of Fathy's beautiful mosque* (above).

For many visitors to Egypt, the greatest attraction of the West Bank at Luxor is the Valley of the Kings, where generation after generation of New Kingdom pharaohs were buried, surrounded by symbols of their wealth. The tombs served as a medium for the kings to pictorially worship the gods whom they expected to meet in the afterlife: a mass of sacred scriptures adorn the walls, and the kings are often portrayed making offerings and fraternizing with the deities. Many tombs were carved out of the rock, with long corridors leading deep into the earth's surface, and many incorporate several different chambers and levels before they lead to the inner sanctum – the burial chamber itself. One of the longest corridors in the Valley of the Kings is in the tomb of Ramesses VI (above). Along its length, hieroglyphs represent the religious books that deal with the concept of birth, life and death as a continuous process. Although many of these books are seen in other tombs in the Valley, this particular tomb has a number that are not found anywhere else, and which therefore provide Egyptologists with a more complete picture of the scriptures. The chamber at the far end of the corridor contains a black granite sarcophagus that once held the mummified remains of Ramesses VI, but this was emptied by grave robbers in antiquity.

In the tomb of Ramesses I, a steep corridor leads to a well-decorated burial chamber. The scripture illustrated in the chamber is the Book of the Gates, and the evocative wall paintings depict the king making offerings to the gods Anubis and Horus (left), among other scenes of dedication and worship.

The Valley of the Kings

In 1922 the Egyptologist Howard Carter, backed by Lord Carnavon, stunned the world with his discovery of a tomb that had managed to escape being plundered – the tomb of Tutankhamun, which has become the most famous of Egyptian tombs in modern times. The young pharaoh's mummified body was encased in a solid gold coffin and two further mummiform coffins; these were surrounded in turn by a stone sarcophagus, which was entombed by four golden shrines, one inside the other. In the adjoining chambers, some 1,700 precious objects were found crammed together, which took almost ten years to be labelled and cleared. The tomb itself is now sadly all but empty, its riches having been taken away to be displayed in the Egyptian Museum in Cairo; the inevitable focal point and most memorable item in the museum exhibition is the death mask of Tutankhamun *(above)*, *which has become as recognizable a symbol of Ancient Egypt as the Pyramids and the Sphinx at Giza.*

Regarded as one of the most impressive of the tombs in the Valley of the Kings, the tomb of Seti I has a complex set of chambers connected by corridors and steps. The exquisite murals depict several of the religious books and many of the deities, with detailed carvings that pick out hairstyles and leopardskin robes in high relief (above right), *and colourful paintings* (right).

The Land of the Nubians
To Lake Nasser and Abu Simbel

From Luxor to Aswan, cruisers and *feluccas* ply the waters of the southern part of the Egyptian Nile at a gentle pace, giving the many visitors to this stretch of the river a glimpse of life in a rural setting peppered with historic monuments. Beyond the riverbank, a different aspect of traditional life also reflects a timeless continuity. Camel traders have always driven great herds of animals northwards across the Nubian Desert from breeding grounds in Sudan to the markets in Egypt. At Daraw a weekly camel market draws traders and herdsmen from Sudan and all parts of the country.

Aswan, on the east bank of the Nile, is the southernmost town in Egypt, lying in the shadow of the Aswan Dam and High Dam. Its market, which runs through the centre of the town, thrives on local and tourist trade, and its traders look forward (and wistfully backward) to extra business when diplomatic relationships with Sudan permit.

The Aswan area exercises a great hold on people's affections. The Agha Khan III was so passionate about the place that after his death in 1957 a mausoleum was built here among the desert sands he loved. It stands on the brow of the West Bank horizon, close to the ruins of St Simeon's Monastery, sharing a vantage point with a row of tombs known as the Tombs of the Nobles. These are carved into the hillside rock at the northern end of the ridge and date from as far back as the Old and Middle Kingdom eras up to and including Roman times.

Aswan's waterfront faces onto the picturesque group of islands and rocks known as the First Cataract of the Nile. When the High Dam was built in the 1960s, creating the massive Lake Nasser, the traditional lands of the Nubians were plunged beneath the water, drowning much of their heritage and their homes but never dampening their spirits. Many were relocated to Elephantine Island, the largest of the islands, which is now one of the last strongholds of Nubian culture, with a quite different atmosphere and architectural style from that of Aswan itself. Other islands were put to different uses: one, given to General Kitchener for leading the Egyptian army to victory over the Sudanese, was turned into a botanical garden that is still maintained today.

South of Aswan, some ancient monuments were rescued before the waters engulfed them. Most were relocated at the edge of the lake, but the Temple of Philae was moved to an island that was sculpted to resemble the submerged original. The most remarkable achievement, however, was the relocation of the temples of Abu Simbel some 300 kilometres (186 miles) south of Aswan. The feat of engineering in this project is as impressive as the Dam itself, and is as astonishing as the achievements of the civilization that built the temples.

The Land of the Nubians

HISTORIC UPPER EGYPT: EDFU AND KOM OMBO

On the edge of the modern-day town of Edfu, the Hypostyle Hall (opposite, above) of the Temple of Horus dates from the reign of Ptolemy VII. A procession of Horus-headed priests ascends to the roof on one mural (right), while a statue of the god watches over visitors in the Court of Offerings (opposite, below). Further south at Kom Ombo, another magnificent Ptolemaic temple is dedicated to the gods Haroeris and Sobek (top and above).

PREVIOUS PAGES
Page 106: *A colossal head of Ramesses II in front of the majestic Sun Temple at Abu Simbel.*
Page 107: *Fishermen at the First Cataract of the Nile.*

The Land of the Nubians

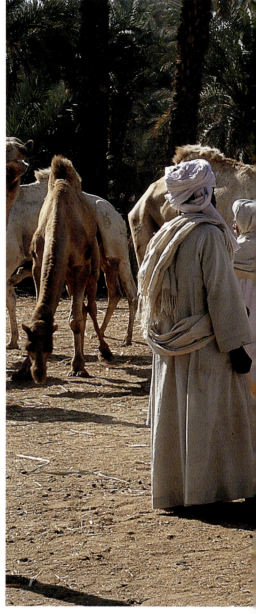

To the south of Kom Ombo lies the village of Daraw, famous for its camel market, where camels are bought and sold every week, attracting traders from all over the country. The market has developed as the last staging post on the long route from Sudan, also called the Forty-Day Road. Nomadic tribesmen from the provinces of Dafur and Kordofan walk their herds in caravans a hundred strong across the deserts, oblivious to intense heat and international boundaries.

Daraw Camel Market

The journey to Daraw from their original homes can take the nomads and camels as long as two or three months. Having walked this extraordinary distance, the groaning and complaining of the camels fills the air as they are loaded onto trucks to continue their journey through Egypt. The next destination is the huge camel market at Birqash, northwest of Cairo, and from there across the Middle East and North Africa, ending up either as beasts of burden or as food.

THE LAND OF THE NUBIANS

THE NILE AT ASWAN

Further down the Nile from Daraw, Aswan, the southernmost city in Egypt, stands on the east bank of the river, overlooking an area of rocks and islands known as the First Cataract of the Nile (left). At any time of day, this expanse of water is populated by feluccas, *the traditional sailing boats of the Nile, and their crews (top);* feluccas *originate from the Aswan region, and many boatbuilders, owners and captains live in and around the city, particularly on the islands of the First Cataract.*

Not only feluccas *can be seen on the river here: children use the water as a playground from an early age, paddling about in tiny, home-made boats (middle), and fishermen earn a living from this well-stocked resource (above).*

ASWAN: THE WEST BANK

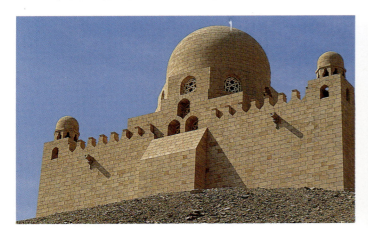

In direct contrast to the lush vegetation of the islands of the First Cataract at Aswan (top), the desert sands of the West Bank of the Nile come right down to the water's edge from a ridge of hills that dominates the horizon. Among these sands 7th-century Christians built St Simeon's Monastery (opposite, below) as a base from which to send missionaries into Nubia; the original buildings were razed and rebuilt in the 12th century. Some 13 centuries after the monks first settled here, the Agha Khan III fell in love with the West Bank sands and adopted Aswan as his second home. After his death in 1957, a mausoleum for his remains (above) was constructed by his widow. Overlooking the Nile from a commanding position (opposite, above), the tomb has become an attraction for thousands of visitors, who come from Aswan or Elephantine Island to the landing stage by traditional felucca *(right).*

The Land of the Nubians

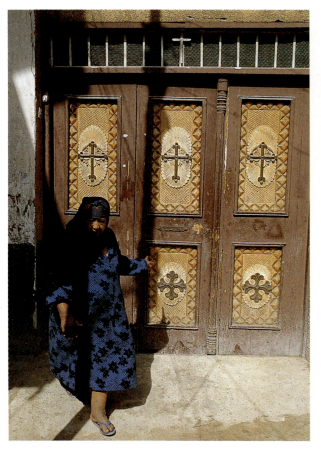

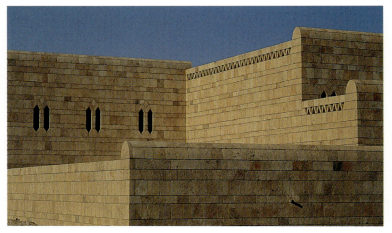

Perhaps the most famous building in modern-day Aswan, the Old Cataract Hotel (top) was built in the Victorian age, during the height of British colonial rule. It opened in 1899, and was then enlarged and modified, culminating in the grand restaurant; the opening of this room in 1902 was attended by the ruler of Egypt, the Khedive Abbas II Hilmi, Lord and Lady Cromer and a young Winston Churchill. A few decades later, Agatha Christie wrote her famous novel Death on the Nile *while she was staying at the hotel.*

Other distinctive, if less visited, forms of architecture in Aswan include the Coptic church (left), tucked away in a backstreet of the city, and the recently completed Nubian Museum (above), intended to be a showcase of Nubian architecture and art.

THE ARCHITECTURE OF ASWAN

As in the rest of the country, the history of Islamic architecture in Aswan spans many centuries. To the south of the city, the ancient Muslim Cemetery (top) is the site of fine examples of mausoleums that use interior domes and arches (right) to complement the mostly cubic construction of the exteriors. The majority of these tombs were built by the Fatimids between the 10th and 12th centuries, although some of the earliest ones go back as far as the 8th century. The Muslim tradition is not confined to architecture and formal art, however, and it is not uncommon to see houses painted with lively folk-art murals, depicting the journey of the householder on a ritual pilgrimage to the holy city of Mecca (above).

THE LAND OF THE NUBIANS

During the construction of the High Dam, to the south of Aswan, in the late 1960s, the rising waters threatened to submerge many of the ancient monuments in their path. One of these, the Temple of Isis (above) on Philae Island, was constructed in the Ptolemaic era and remained a cult site through the Roman and early Christian periods. After the building of the first dam, the temple was semi-submerged by the tidal river waters for part of each year, and it became clear during the building of the new dam that it would become submerged once and for all. An international rescue project was launched by UNESCO, and the entire temple complex was relocated between 1972 and 1980 to the neighbouring, higher island of Aglika, which was landscaped to resemble Philae. The ornate Kiosk of Trajan (left), one of the last pieces to be rescued, was brought up by divers from the British Navy, and the project saved many other magnificent monuments, such as the Lion Statue in the Temple of Isis (opposite), from disappearing forever beneath the waters.

THE ISLAND OF PHILAE

LAKE NASSER

The completion of the Aswan High Dam in 1971 created the world's biggest man-made lake – Lake Nasser *(above)*, which stretches some 500 kilometres (300 miles) beyond Aswan itself and past the border with Sudan, where the old town of Wadi Halfa was engulfed. In addition to Philae, several more remote monuments were rescued and brought to the edge of the advancing lake. The Kiosk of Qirtasi *(opposite)*, which has a similar age and appearance to the Kiosk of Trajan, originally came from a site further south of Aswan. Egypt has benefited greatly from the dam – the irrigation that it provides has made it possible for vast areas of land to be used for agriculture, and hydroelectric generators, powered by the waters of Lake Nasser, have been a valuable source of energy for the country. However, the long-term effects of the dam are only now being discovered, and serious doubts about its environmental sustainability have arisen.

Though many years have passed since Lake Nasser was created, the desert still comes down to the edge of its waters. No green fringe has developed, and the abandoned mechanical cranes that helped rescue the ancient monuments are now almost submerged themselves *(middle right)*, bringing a surreal atmosphere to this vast open space. The main losers in the short term were the Nubians: where there was once a land with history, culture and 120,000 villagers, today there is only a huge surface of water and the occasional fisherman *(below right)*.

The Land of the Nubians

When the Nubians were resettled after losing their traditional homelands under the waters of Lake Nasser, many made their new homes in West Bank villages (above) and among the islands of the First Cataract of the Nile at Aswan. On the West Bank, the farmers manage to sustain a traditional lifestyle (left), using a form of agriculture that still draws its water using turbines powered by animals (opposite, below left). The largest of the islands, Elephantine Island, has become something akin to a capital of the new Nubia – even though it is now under threat from the modern world. Elephantine is little more than 2 kilometres (1.25 miles) long and about 500 metres (1,900 feet) at its widest point; the ruins of the ancient city of Abu take up the southern part, and the Aswan Oberoi Hotel and other new developments occupy the northern end of the island. Despite this, in two Nubian villages, housing about 2,200 people, the narrow streets (opposite, top) and the traditionally constructed and painted houses (opposite, below right) reflect the architectural heritage of the Nubian people.

Nubian Scenes

Nubian Scenes

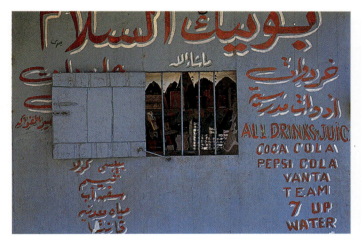

The Nubians are by no means confined to Elephantine Island, but have become a part of the greater population in the city of Aswan, and in the towns and villages that surround it. Their new domain is mainly in the region that stretches north from Aswan to Kom Ombo, although a proportion of the Nubian people has inevitably filtered through to the rest of Egypt, up to and even beyond Cairo. In the south, the land of the Nubians encompasses a world of colourful limewashed mud-brick buildings (opposite) and the courtyard style of a Nubian village on the West Bank (top). In the local stores, window-shopping for cooling drinks takes on a literal meaning (above). The Nubian people have managed to retain their separate ethnic identity, and their features remain distinctly different from those of the wider Egyptian population (right).

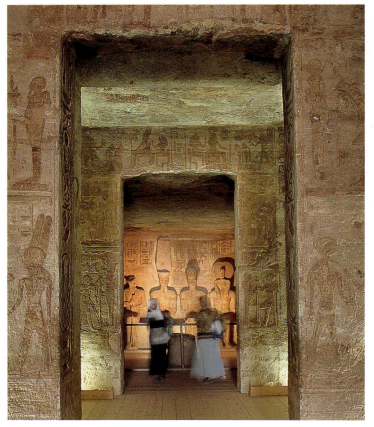

The temples of Abu Simbel (above) represent a remarkable construction achievement of both ancient and modern times. Situated 300 kilometres (186 miles) south of Aswan, the temples were carved into the rock of a mountainside, and were destined to a watery grave with the creation of Lake Nasser. They were precisely aligned so that the sun would penetrate the inner sanctum of the Temple of Ramesses II on the anniversary dates of 22 February and 22 October, illuminating the seated statues of the four gods (left). In addition, the ancient achievement included the colossal construction of the Hypostyle Hall, with its statues of Ramesses II (above left) and its complex carved reliefs (opposite, below left), and the four 20-metre (65-foot) high colossi of the pharaoh on the façade (opposite, below right). The modern achievement was to cut the Sun Temple, and the accompanying Temple of Queen Nefertari, into massive blocks and reassemble them on a hollow dome of concrete, cleverly landscaped to create an exact replica of the original mountain.

Abu Simbel: Temples and Colossi

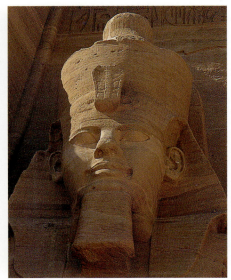

Oases and Sand Dunes
The Western Desert

To the far west of Cairo and the fertile Nile Valley, an area of sand dunes and depressions stretches some 700 kilometres (435 miles) to the south. The most remote oasis to the west, close to the Libyan border, is Siwah, where the rising water table and fresh water springs nourish date palms and aid agriculture in the immediate area. The people of Siwah pride themselves on having maintained a close-knit community that is almost independent of the rest of Egypt. Although they speak a Berber-derived tongue called Siwi, they are in fact neither Berbers nor Bedouins, but Siwans. They have maintained their own unique culture and heritage, demonstrated by the swathes of flowing cotton clothing and heavy silver jewellery of the women.

The people of Siwah have resisted raids and colonization over the centuries, and only became part of Egypt when forced to by Muhammad Ali's troops in 1820. This isolation has long bestowed a near-legendary status on Siwah, and the oasis was a point of pilgrimage for Alexander the Great in 331 BC, when he came to consult the 'Oracle of Amun', situated in the temple of the now-ruined town of Aghurmi.

The most breathtaking features in the vast Western Desert are its geological features. Just to the south of Siwah, the Great Sand Sea stretches for hundreds of miles, with dunes like waves of sand some 100 metres (328 feet) high, that can be anything up to 50 kilometres (31 miles) long. Between the palm-groved settlements at Bahriyyah and Farafrah is the White Desert, an area dominated by extraordinary white limestone monoliths that rise from the desert floor. Over the centuries, the rock has been eroded into huge, surreal sculptures until it resembles an eerie art gallery on a grand scale.

The four other oases of the Western Desert – Bahriyyah, Farafrah, Dakhlah and Khargah – where Bedouins and Berbers settled by valuable water sources, are known as the inner circle of oases. Sited in depressions below the main plateau of the desert floor, they are characterized by traditional mud-brick houses. Dakhlah, south of Farafrah, is one of the biggest of the oasis areas, but is not confined to a single spot. It is made up of some 14 separate settlements that support a population of around 65,000; the layouts and many of the buildings in the largest of these towns, Mut and Al-Qasr, date back to the Mamluk era.

In contrast, Khargah has nearly as great a population, but the majority of the people in this oasis live in a single modern city, Al-Khargah. Here the old mud-brick houses have been swept away for new development, in a New Valley project that is planned to increase the habitable lands of Egypt. Whatever the surroundings, the oasis towns are all transformed into riots of colour during the *moulid* festivities.

Oases and Sand Dunes

In the far north-west of Egypt's Western Desert, close to the border with Libya, stands the oasis of Siwah. Nestling in splendid isolation between the Qattarah Depression and the Great Sand Sea, the principal town, also called Siwah, and the neighbouring old town of Aghurmi (above) have survived almost independently of the rest of the country for centuries. The mud-brick houses of the oasis (left) are uncomplicated structures, simple dwellings made from kharsif, hard-setting mud gathered from around the salty lakes. They provide basic shelter from the harsh desert conditions but are eroded easily by rainfall, giving even the best or most recently built a crumbling look. Electricity reached the community of Siwah only recently, but it is already changing the landscape – power lines crisscross the skyline, and an incongruous air of modernity glares out of the local barber's and other occasional shop fronts that are sandwiched between older building styles (below left).

PREVIOUS PAGES
Page 128: *The massive sand dunes of the Great Sand Sea.*
Page 129: *Mosque interior at Al-Qasr, Dakhlah Oasis.*

130

Siwah, Remote and Lush Oasis

The old fortified centre of Siwah, known as Shali (the Berber Siwi word for 'town'), was founded at the beginning of the 13th century after the waters of the old town of Aghurmi became poisonous and its inhabitants moved out. The remains of Aghurmi's walls and chimneys dominate the landscape to this day, like the remnants of a washed-out sandcastle (right). In the early 20th century, Shali was abandoned in its turn after a disastrous series of rainstorms that began to destroy its buildings.

New buildings are now appearing in the centre of Siwah, but many of the sleepy outlying streets (top) look as though they could have been imported directly from Aghurmi. The low, sun-baked structures, whether inhabited by families or used as workshops by blacksmiths and other craftsmen (above), retain a traditional character.

Oases and Sand Dunes

Most of the inhabitants of the Siwah Oasis eke out a simple living from the land and follow a self-sufficient lifestyle, which could potentially lead to the isolation of individuals and families. But rather than falling foul of this isolation, the people of Siwah have developed an extraordinarily strong community spirit, which is best seen in the way that the population turns out for the religious festivals, the moulids *(above right). This was not always the case, however: until the early part of this century, inter-tribal fighting and battles between villages were common, until the differences were settled and the October* moulid, *held at the time of the full moon, was chosen to celebrate the new sense of unity. During the* moulid, *large crowds of men gather together in makeshift mosques (top left), then, at midday, assemble for prayers on open ground, facing in the direction of Mecca – marked by anything from a* mihrab, *or mosque niche, to an umbrella – and pray (above left).*

THE OCTOBER *MOULID* AT SIWAH

Unlike the moulids *in the large urban areas, where food stalls compete to cater for the festival-goers, in Siwah the emphasis of the Corban Bairam (Greater Feast) during the festivities is on communal meals. Many camels are slaughtered, and huge cooking pots (opposite, below) are used to make the stews that are shared between the men, boys and young girls (right) – the women and adolescent girls must stay in their homes during the* moulid.

Oases and Sand Dunes

The people of the oasis towns and villages around Siwah travel for many miles to get to the three-day October moulid (opposite, above), and stay there for the duration of the festival before making the long journey home. Most rely on the traditional donkey and cart to get there (above), and their arrival transforms a normally quiet district near the town into one big party area. Even though the preparations for the festival may have been going on for months, stalls appear as if out of nowhere, selling ice creams (left), large, brightly coloured balloons (opposite, below) and tartours, conical party hats (below left), to the excited children.

The October *Moulid* at Siwah

Oases and Sand Dunes

THE GREAT SAND SEA

South of the Siwah Oasis is the area known as the Great Sand Sea, an ocean of sand with dunes 100 metres (328 feet) high, which has been an obstacle to exploration and land navigation for centuries. One of the first recorded expeditions to discover its extent took place in 1874, when Rohlfs set off with 17 camels, but after just 18 days they began to die from lack of water. He was forced to abandon his westbound route along the mighty dunes, and headed north towards Siwah along the valleys between them. After this, it was not until 1923 that the western edge of the Sand Sea was discovered by an Egyptian, Hassanein Bey, on an extraordinary camel journey from the Mediterranean to the western provinces of Sudan. Archeological excavations within the region have uncovered evidence of Neolithic hunter-gatherers who lived in this area at a time when it was green savannah; today, the massive dunes and strange geological formations are a stark reminder of the powers of nature to change a landscape beyond all recognition.

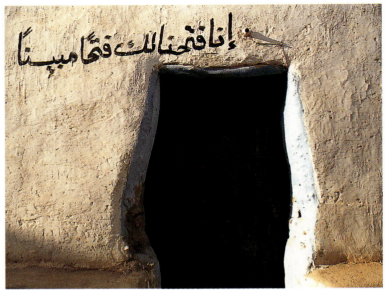

The route that skirts the Great Sand Sea, heading south-east from Siwah, leads to the Bahriyyah Oasis, sometimes referred to as the Northern Oasis. Bahriyyah is only 360 kilometres (223 miles) from Cairo, making it far less isolated, but the rough terrain makes for a long journey. Like Siwah, it is a true oasis, relying for its very existence on the spring waters that miraculously surface through the arid, rocky land – there is almost no rainfall at all here. The oasis area covers some 2,000 square kilometres (772 square miles) of a natural depression, and is home to a mass of palm and olive groves.

Within the Bahriyyah Oasis there are several villages and the main town, Bawiti. They are all characterized by traditional mud-brick dwellings, often with calligraphic inscriptions that provide a visual focal point among the otherwise blank façades (above).

Bahriyyah, the Northern Oasis

Over the years, the people of the Bahriyyah Oasis have been influenced by historic events that originated outside their close-knit communities. Despite their Christian heritage, dating from the 4th century, they were among the first groups to convert to Islam when the Muslims took power in the country in the 7th century. Three centuries later the Bahriyyah region became an independent Berber emirate, but this did not last long and the area was reclaimed into the greater Egyptian fold in the 12th century. Regardless of these external influences, it appears that the community has suffered little dilution of its identity, and is still made up of the same independent oasis inhabitants as it has always been. In fact, even the livestock of Bahriyyah has changed little over time – the cows that are driven through the narrow streets (opposite, below) bear a remarkable resemblance to those depicted on ancient reliefs, and are a breed found nowhere else in Egypt.

OASES AND SAND DUNES

Travelling south-west again from Bahriyyah, the road runs alongside the White Desert just before it reaches the next oasis, Farafrah. The unique and bizarre landscape of this area has been hewn out of the dazzling white limestone rocks by aeons of wind erosion. The strange geological shapes thus created are like a surreal moonscape, changing colour with every passing hour, according to the angle of the daylight or moonlight. With the recent growth of the oasis region as a tourist destination, travellers can visit the edges of the White Desert by car or bus, and four-wheel-drive vehicles and drivers can be hired from the Farafrah or Bahriyyah oases to make daytime or overnight journeys into the very heart of this unforgettable desert (right).

The White Desert

Oases and Sand Dunes

The popularity and habitation of the oasis towns seems to come and go like the ever-changing sands of the deserts that surround them. In the Dakhlah Oasis region, several town have sprung into prominence at different periods: the old capital of the area was Al-Qasr, a town in the north of the lush oasis, which was founded during the Roman era. It continued to grow after the Muslim invasion, and the distinctive minaret of the mosque (above) was added during the reign of the Ayyubids in the 12th century. Al-Qasr's pre-eminence in the oasis did not last, however; Mut, to the south, overtook it in population and importance, and most of the old town is uninhabited, with just a few hundred people where once there were thousands. A few crafts are still practised here, such as pottery (above left), and the crumbling old dwellings (opposite, below) and Muslim tombs, with their intricate carved lintels (opposite, above), are quite typical examples of oasis architecture.

North-west of the Dakhla Oasis, and a starting point for exploring the White Desert, Farafrah Oasis is the smallest of the Western Desert oases. Until new roads were constructed, the only town, Al-Qasr al-Farafrah, was off the tourist route and saw few visitors; the townsfolk are still able to shut out the outside world with an intense game of backgammon outside a café (left).

Oases and Sand Dunes

On the southern edge of the Dakhlah Oasis, the town of Mut is surrounded by hot sulphur springs that are popular with visitors and also prove irresistible to the local children (above left). The old town area is dominated by a ruined citadel, now completely uninhabited, which offers commanding views of the new town to the north and the desert to the south. The pace of life around Mut is gentle, as one would expect in a region where agriculture is the main occupation – the streets and alleyways of the outskirts of the town are quiet thoroughfares, with pedestrians and traditional donkey carts the main traffic to be seen (left).

Dakhlah Oasis: Around Mut

For most of the time, the peace in the countryside around Mut is only broken by the bleating of a herd of goats, kicking up the dust on the old roads as they are driven along (above). Wheat, rice and fruit are the principal crops in the area, grown and harvested in fields where modern irrigation may have provided the water, but where traditional practices still hold sway in a timeless scene of Egyptian rural life (right).

Oases and Sand Dunes

Like the other oases of the Western Desert, Khargah Oasis, the largest and furthest south, has benefited from the New Valley scheme, which has aimed since the late 1950s to greatly increase the agricultural land of the oases in a number of ways. In the case of Khargah, some of the old springs and wells that had served the oasis for centuries were beginning to dry up, threatening the very existence of the main town, Al-Khargah; new pumps and bores provided by the scheme reversed the trend, and brought a new lushness to the area (right).

With a population of nearly 75,000, Al-Khargah is a thriving town where the growing tourist industry is balanced by the traditional oasis lifestyles and occupations of its people. Street traders play an important part in daily life, with fruit and vegetable sellers (top) among the many market stalls, and travelling fuul sellers, who provide the staple breakfast and snack from handcarts (above).

Khargah, the Largest Oasis

Oases and Sand Dunes

AROUND AL-KHARGAH

Along the edges of the narrow Khargah Oasis, the desert sands have encroached on once-occupied and thriving land, engulfing towns, temples and tombs from bygone eras. One relatively unscathed site, the Necropolis of al-Baqawat (opposite, above), is a collection of Christian tombs to the north of Al-Khargah, dating from the 3rd to the 7th centuries. The decoration of the small chapels above many of the 263 tombs was influenced by Roman architecture: classical columns and arches adorn the doorways, and several structures even incorporate complex vaulting, despite being made of mud bricks. At the nearby Temple of Amun among the few remaining ruins of the ancient town of Hibis (opposite, below), a combination of desert sands and palm-grove landscapes surrounds the site. The temple dates from the 6th century BC, during the 26th Dynasty, and is one of the few examples of Ancient Egyptian architecture from the Persian period to have remained reasonably well preserved.

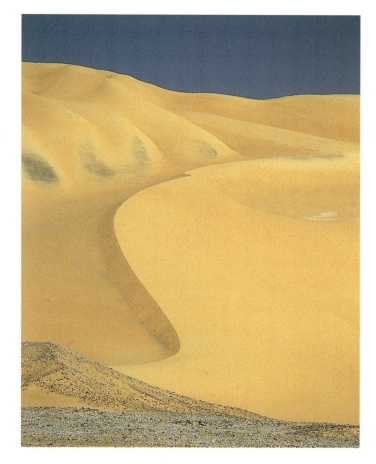

Other ancient structures have fared less well, and little is left of another 26th-Dynasty temple, the Qasr al-Ghuwaydah, a few kilometres to the south of Al-Khargah (above). As the massive sand dunes continue to be shifted by the winds of the desert (right), the boundaries of the oases are always changing.

The Red Sea Coast and Sinai Peninsula

Bedouin Hinterland and Undersea Paradise

Crossing the Nile from the Western Desert, it is only a matter of a few kilometres across the green cultivation and the waters of the Nile Valley to the Eastern Desert. From here, the land between the river and the Red Sea coast is broken only by the peaks of the majestic Red Sea Mountain range.

The Eastern Desert stretches down to the sea, making life on the coast difficult to support. There is vrtually no natural fresh water here, and large towns such as Hurghadah are dependent on desalination plants and piped water from the Nile. Despite this, developments are cropping up all along this coast, in the hope of creating new resorts for tourists.

The main attraction in this area is the Red Sea itself, where rich coral reef ecosystems lie just beneath the water. The marine life is so rich and exquisite that it has become a must for any diver. Some of the most exciting spots for diving can be reached from the mainland resorts, while others are accessible from across the water by way of the Sinai Peninsula resorts. Sharm al-Shaykh is well placed for sites both in the Gulf of Aqabah and the Straits of Gubal, which lies between Hurghadah and Sharm, marking the area where the open sea is channelled into the Gulf of Suez. Many a ship has come to grief here, lending an added attraction to underwater exploration.

North of Hurghadah, on the way to Suez, are the Red Sea Monasteries. Hidden in the barren hills, these remote enclaves represent some of the earliest vestiges of Egypt's Christian heritage. In this part of the country, the diversity of Egypt's history is brought home time and again. Just a few hours away from these ancient monasteries, the Suez Canal has dominated the country's more recent history, not just because of its strategic importance for global navigation, but as a border with the Sinai peninsula over which wars have been fought with Israel in a struggle for possession of the territory.

Crossing into Sinai, it is hard to imagine the land as a battlefield – in small settlements, Bedouins exist as they have for centuries. Their semi-nomadic lives are little changed, except that there is now a market for their traditional crafts, and they bring their embroidery, camel bags and silver jewellery to sell in the weekly Bedouin market at the Mediterranean coastal resort of Al-Arish.

The Sinai hills have a mystical quality, enchanting and spiritually evocative. The early Scriptures placed Mount Sinai as the setting for the Burning Bush and the site where Moses received the Ten Commandments. Today the mountain draws pilgrims from all over the world, to visit St Catherine's Monastery at its base and to climb and view the magical sunrise from its summit.

The Red Sea Coast and Sinai Peninsula

Journeying east from the oasis towns in the Western Desert, the traveller crosses the Nile Valley and is almost immediately confronted by the rocky Eastern Desert, dominated by the magnificent Red Sea Mountains (opposite, below right). The oldest known route through the mountains goes from Qift on the Nile to Al-Qusayr on the Red Sea coast, one of the few towns along the eastern coastline to have a historical significance. In pharaonic times it was a major port, providing communication and trade routes with the Middle East and Africa's east coast ports, and it was the largest Muslim port of the Red Sea until the 10th century. Today it is a small town that derives most of its revenue from phosphate extraction, though there are still plenty of old-style buildings that provide the town with its architectural character (above), and the inhabitants are proud to display the mausoleums of once-prominent local sheiks (left). More common along this stretch of coastline are the towns that have grown over recent decades. Hurghadah, the largest, originated as a fishing village, and fishermen's boats (opposite, top) still operate from its shoreline. However, a huge influx of tourism has led to massive developments of modern hotels and resorts that offer diving boats for underwater explorers (opposite, middle left). The uncongested road past Hurghadah is flanked by concrete structures and hoardings advertising the resort facilities (opposite, below left).

PREVIOUS PAGES
Page 150: *Camel-owner at the foot of Mount Sinai.*
Page 151: *Bedouin woman from the Sinai Peninsula in traditional Bedouin costume.*

Along the Red Sea Coast

The Red Sea Coast and Sinai Peninsula

With a spectacular variety of undersea sights in their waters – extensive, thriving coral gardens, mysterious caves, sheer walls and an immense variety of fish and other marine creatures – the Red Sea and Gulfs of Aqabah and Suez are major destinations for divers. Once in the crystal clear, warm waters, divers are rewarded with a multitude of striking, colourful views: solitary Blotched Bigeyes (above, middle) and striped Emperor Angelfish (above) swimming deep among the hard corals, and miniature, jewel-like Fairy Basslets darting in and out of the waving soft corals (right). South of the dive centres off the shores of Hurghadah and Al-Qusayr, the world-class dive sites of Rocky Island and the two tiny islands that make up The Brothers are reached from the deep south coast (top).

The Red Sea Coast and Sinai Peninsula

Ranging from sheer cliff faces to gently undulating floors, the coral reefs below the placid surface in the Straits of Tiran (above), between the south Sinai coast and Tiran Island, are home to hard and soft corals, sharks, dolphins, rusting and coral-covered wrecks of all sizes, and a marvellous variety of coral reef fishes. To the east of Tiran Island, the town of Sharm al-Shaykh is the major diving centre on the Sinai Peninsula (opposite, below right). From here, beginners learn the rudiments of diving, and experts and marine photographers from around the world head for the sites around the national park of Ras Muhammad, on the southern tip of the peninsula.

The smallest of the marine turtles, the Hawksbill Turtle, is a frequent visitor to the unpolluted seas around the coral reefs, and a highlight of any dive in the area is the chance to swim alongside one (left).

Marine Wonders of the Red Sea

The surreal landscapes of the undersea world around the Sinai coast are home to a fantastic array of marine life. Grey, Hammerhead and Blacktip sharks and other pelagic fish, such as barracudas and jacks, come to feed on smaller reef fish, and dolphins are sometimes seen. In addition to these larger sea dwellers, there is a whole world of beautiful miniature creatures. With close observation, tiny Spider Crabs can be seen clinging onto soft Dendronephthya coral, where they make their homes (bottom left), and shoals of silvery Glassfish swim through swaying sea fans (right).

Just one of the many varieties of starfish species in the reefs around the Red Sea and the Gulfs, Common Starfish live among hard coral rubble (below) – the elongated arm will eventually separate from the the body and begin to form a new starfish.

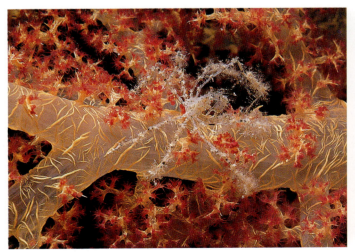

Hidden in the hills that overlook the Gulf of Suez are the two Red Sea Monasteries of St Paul and St Anthony – the country's oldest monasteries. St Paul was an Egyptian Christian who fled from Alexandria during the persecutions of the 3rd century; he lived a hermit's life in a cave in these mountains, and his followers built the monastery after his death. The buildings have been raided, ransacked and nearly destroyed in their long life, but periods of restoration have always preserved them and provided continuity with the early Church. They remain an important centre for Copts (left), although certain areas, like the old press room (above), have been retained as a museum. The murals that adorn the chapels are fine examples of the bold Coptic style (top).

Travelling north from the Red Sea coast, the second monastery to be reached is St Anthony's (above). This is a much bigger complex than the neighbouring St Paul's, and includes houses, market gardens, mills and five churches (top). This monastery has always overshadowed St Paul's, mirroring the spiritual superiority of St Anthony, the founder of the Desert Fathers and Christian monasticism in general, and the man who convinced Paul of his own saintliness. Today it continues to support a thriving monastic community (right).

The Red Sea Coast and Sinai Peninsula

From its very conception, the Suez Canal has caused political divisions as well as the physical division of mainland Africa from the Sinai Peninsula and Middle East. Its opening in 1869 created one of the world's busiest shipping routes, providing a link from Europe to the East without having to circumnavigate the African continent; in the south, what was once a peaceful fishing area is now transformed into a highway for massive container ships (above). *The canal also inadvertently created a potential international boundary, leading to renewed disputes over the ownership of the Sinai Peninsula, which effectively became cut off from the rest of Egypt. Even today, relics of these disputes can be seen, remnants of war like the captured Israeli tanks in the town of Ismailiyyah* (left). *The town suffered considerably from Israeli bombardment during the conflicts of the 1960s and 1970s, but has been largely restored to the European-style garden city that it was under colonial occupation, when Ismailiyyah was the headquarters of the internationally owned Suez Canal Company.*

North of Ismailiyyah, the ferry that crosses the canal at Qantarah (below left) *provided one of the few links with Sinai before the construction of the Ahmad Hamdi Tunnel. In many ways Sinai is like a separate country with its own traditional occupants, the Bedouins, who have led desert lives quite independent of the political goings-on around them. To an extent they have also managed to preserve their culture, and one of the best places to encounter this is at the Bedouin market at Al-Arish* (opposite).

The Red Sea Coast and Sinai Peninsula

The largest town in the Sinai Peninsula and the capital of the North Sinai province, Al-Arish is situated right on the Mediterranean coast, close to Egypt's border with Israel. Although it is a thriving resort town that attracts Egyptian holidaymakers to its beaches, it is perhaps best visited for its markets (opposite, above). Being the main town, it acts as a magnet for people from throughout the region, who come to trade all manner of wares (opposite, below) and to meet and relax (below).

The Bedouins lead a largely nomadic life, herding sheep and goats on whatever sparse grazing they can find in this arid land; the Bedouin market at Al-Arish is one of the few places where they can gather, bringing their sheep as one of their rare tradable commodities (below left). Traditionally dressed Bedouin women stand out among the crowds, wearing black headscarves, heavy silver or beaten-metal jewellery, and leather or fabric veils that partially cover their faces (left).

AL-ARISH BEDOUIN MARKET

THE SINAI INTERIOR

Sinai's interior is a rich landscape of spectacular rocky mountain scenery interspersed with plateaus of desert, dried river valleys – the wadis that once ran with water (above) – and hidden green valleys where rivers still run today. It is a land of extraordinary natural beauty, where inquisitive travellers go camel-trekking or on Jeep safaris to find the unexpected – surreal scenes like the Coloured Canyon in the east (opposite), or a seemingly private Bedouin moulid (top). Although it has been referred to as a wilderness since Biblical times, it is clear that many a civilization has made Sinai its home, and the Bedouins still think of it as such. The community that once worshipped at the Temple of Hathor at Sarabit al-Khadim abandoned the area in the reign of Ramesses VII, and all that remains of this lofty rock temple from the 12th Dynasty are some inscribed stelae (right).

The Red Sea Coast and Sinai Peninsula

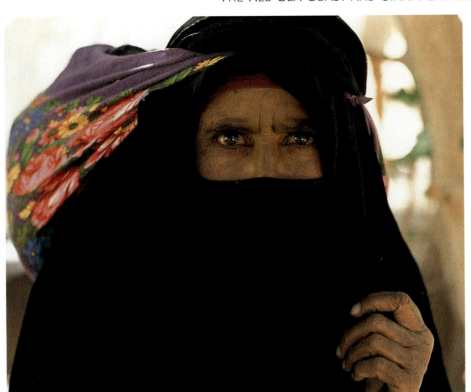

A number of Bedouin tribes live in Sinai, and although the essence of their traditional way of life is centred on their being a nomadic population, the extent of their wanderings is limited. Each of the tribes has claimed an area of Sinai as their own, and they stay for the most part within these recognized, though ill-defined, boundaries. Most of the Bedouins claim to be pure Arabs, although one tribe, the Jabalyyah, who live around St Catherine's Monastery, claim an ancestry that emanated from Caucasia, an area between the Black and the Caspian Seas. The true origins of the 27 tribes may be lost in the mists of time and legend, but collectively they have a shared Bedouin lifestyle. Black headscarves and veils are common to all women, and the black tents are as ubiquitous to a Bedouin settlement as the herds of goats, sheep and camels on which they live.

The Bedouins

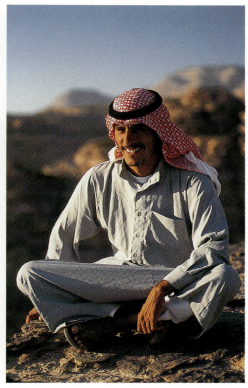

Scenes from Bedouin Life

Animals play a large role in the traditional way of life of the Bedouins, and much of their working day involves looking after their herds as they graze (opposite, above). Even when coaxed into leaving their nomadic lifestyle for settlement in semi-permanent houses, they still take their livestock into the new environment (opposite, below). This settlement is in the wadi of Ain Koudra, which has been a valuable source of water for centuries. Although it appears barren and arid for much of the year, it is an oasis with a fresh water spring that brings life-giving sustenance to the Bedouins and their herds.

The real mark of a Bedouin's wealth is the number of camels that his family or tribe possesses. The most valuable camels of all are the hageen, the racing camels (above). Camel-racing is still a favourite sport of these desert-dwellers, who have an extraordinary ability to handle the beasts, persuading them to become high-speed, high-performance racers. Other communities which use camels seem to have trouble getting them even to be slow-moving beasts of burden, but this is second nature to the Bedouins. Arab horses, with their distinctive build and elegant features, are no strangers to the deserts of Sinai; they wear their elaborate, decorated saddlery with pride, and respond instantly to the commands of expert horsemen (right).

St Catherine's Monastery

St Catherine's Monastery, which nestles at the foot of Mount Sinai in the southern interior of the Sinai Peninsula, is an active monastery occupied by Greek Orthodox monks. The site was chosen because the scriptures suggest that this was the place of the Burning Bush, from which Moses heard the voice of God. St Catherine's was founded in 337, at the instigation of the Byzantine Empress Helena; the church in the centre of the complex was built between 542 and 551, and additions were made throughout the centuries, perhaps the most notable being the 18th-century ceiling. The relics of the martyr St Catherine were only brought to the site during the Crusades, when they were uncovered at Mount Catherine, Egypt's highest peak, a few kilometres south of Mount Sinai.

The Red Sea Coast and Sinai Peninsula

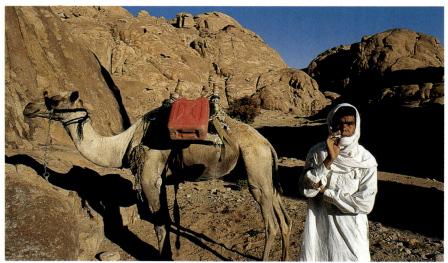

St Catherine's is as much a site for pilgrimage today as it has been in the past. Mount Sinai, which stands directly behind the monastery, is the mountain where Moses is supposed to have been given the Ten Commandments, and even to the non-religious it is a site of extraordinary beauty. Camel-owners wait along the path to offer their services to tourists and pilgrims struggling up the long switchback track to the summit (left); a shorter, but even more arduous route, known as the Steps of Repentance, involves tackling the sheer climb from the monastery on the 3750 steps hewn into the rock by a penitent monk.

Mount Sinai

The visitors come in their thousands, to ascend the mountain and reach the small chapel on its summit (right). *It is a sacred site for Christians, Jews and Muslims alike, and a spiritual place for non-believers. The most potent experience, however, is to spend the night on this 2285-metre (7495-foot) peak* (above), *and to feel the chill mountain air and the warmth of the morning sun as it rises and casts shadows and rays of orange and golden light across this magical land.*

Index

Page numbers in **bold** type refer to illustrations.

Abbasid dynasty 22
Abdu, Fifi 29
Abu Simbel 107, **126-8**
  Hypostyle Hall **126**
  Ramesses II Colossi 30, **109**
  Temple of Queen Nefertari **126**
  Temple of Ramesses II 21, **109**, **126**
Abydos 21, 77, **86-7**
  Temple of Seti I **87**
Acre 23
Acropora coral 15
Africa 11, 12, 13, 14, **160**
Afro-Asian Arabs 16, **16**
Agha Khan III mausoleum 107, **115**
Aghurmi 129, **130**, **131**
agriculture 12, 13, **13**, 14, 21, 27, **42**, 61, 62, 77, **78**, **79**, **94**, 103, 122, **144-5**
Ahmad Hamdi tunnel 12, **160**
Ain Koudra *wadi* **169**
Ain Sukhna 28
Akhenaten, Pharoah 20, **20**, 90
Alabaster Mosque *see* Muhammad Ali Mosque, Cairo
Al-Alamayn 24
Alexander the Great 21, 72, 129
Alexandria 12, 14, 18, 21, **21**, 22, 23, 26, 31, 32, 61, **71-3**
  the library 21, **72**
  Old Arab Quarter **62**, **71**
  Roman Theatre **71**
Amenophis I, Pharoah 20
Amenophis III, Pharoah 20, 30, 77, **97**
Amenophis IV *see* Akhenaten
Amosis, Pharoah 20
Amr, General 17, 22
Amun 20, **20**, 90, **149**
Ancient Egypt 14, 15, 18, 19-22, 29-30, 33, 37, **40-42**, 61, **69**, 77, **82**, **86-7**, **90-92**, **98-9**, **100**, **104-5**, 107, **137**, **149**, **152**
Anfushi Bay, Alexandria **73**
Anubis **98**, **99**, **104**
appliqué work 31, **58**
Arab Republic of Egypt 25
Arabian Desert *see* Eastern Desert
Arab-Israeli war, 1967 25, **160**
architecture 17, 19, 20, 21, 23, **23**, 29-30, **31**, **38**, **40**, 41, **53**, 61, **68**, **69**, **71**, 77, **82**, **84**, **90**, **117**, **122**, **125**, **130**, **131**, **138**, **142**, **149**, **152**
Al-Arish 151, **160**, **162**
the arts 20, 21, **22**, 28-31, **42**, 77, **82**, **87**, **92**, **98**, **101**
Al-Ashmunayn **82**
Asia 12, 13
Assyria 21
Aswan **10**, 15, 17, 34, 107, **113-25**
  First Cataract 13, 17, 30, 107, **109**, **113**, **122**
  Muslim Cemetery **117**
  Old Cataract Hotel **116**
Aswan Dam 12, 13, 27, 107

High Dam 12, 13, 15, 17, 25, 27, 107, **118**, **121**
  see also Lake Nasser
Atlantic Ocean 12
el-Atrach, Farid 29
Ayyub dynasty 22-3, **142**
al-Azhar 17, 22

Bab Zuwaylah gate, Cairo **53**, **58**
baboons 82
Bahri Mamluks 23
Bahriyyah Oasis 129, **138-9**, **140**
Banha 32
Bani Hasan rock tombs **82**
barracudas 15, **157**
Bawiti, Bahriyyah Oasis **138**
Bayt al-Sihaymi, Cairo **53**
beaches and coastal areas 12, 14, 16, 61, **66**, **71**, **73**, 151, **152**, **154-7**, **162**
Bedouin Arabs 16, **16**, 29, **29**, 34, 77, 129, 151, **160**, **162**, **165-9**
belly-dancing 29
Ben Ezra Synagogue, Cairo 18, 37
Berbers 17, 18, 129, **139**
Bey, Hassanein **137**
Biblical times 13, 17, 18, 151, **158**, **165**, 170, **172**
bird species 14, 15
Birket Qarun 14, 77, **78**
Birqash **111**
Blacktip Shark 15, **157**
Blotched Bigeye **154**
Bohra Muslims 17
bommies coral 15
Britain 13, 18, 23-5, 28, 118
bronze casting 31
The Brothers islands, Red Sea **154**
buffalo 14
building materials 30, **31**, **40**, **41**, **67**, **84**, **103**, **125**, 129, **130**, **138**, **149**
Burgi Mamluks 23
business activities 11, 17, 18
Byzantine Christianity 18
Byzantine Empire 21, 31

cabbage coral 15
cafés and restaurants **34**, 35, **54**, **73**, **89**, **94**, **142**
Cairo **5**, **11**, 12, 14, 17, 18, 21, 22, **23**, 26, **34**, 37, **38-60**
  Cities of the Dead 37, **49**
  Islamic Cairo 30, 37, **54-7**
  Khan-al-Khalili **35**, 37, **54-7**
  Old Cairo 18, 30, **46**
calèshe carriages 14, **89**
camel bags 34, 151
camel-racing **169**
camels 14, 16, 107, **110-11**, **133**, **150**, **165**, **166**, **169**, **172**
Camp David Agreement, 1977 25
Caracal 15
Carnavon, Lord **105**
carpets 33-4
Carter, Howard **105**
cat family 15

catfish 14
Central Mosque *see* Muhammad Ali Mosque, Cairo
children **38**, **45**, **58**, **78**, **84**, **113**, **133**, **134**, **144**, **176**
Christianity 17-18, **18**, 21, 22, 30, 37, **46**, 61, **74-5**, 107, **115**, **139**, 151, **158-9**, **170**
Christie, Agatha **116**
churches and monasteries 4, 17, 18, 20, 37, 61, **62**, **74-5**, 77, **84**, 107, **115**, **116**, 151, **158-9**, **166**, **170-73**
cinema 45
the Citadel, Cairo 22, 24, 37, **48**
Cleopatra VII 21
climatic conditions 14
Clownfish 15
colonial rule 18, 24-5, **25**, 28, 31, 61, **72**, **116**, **160**
Colossi of Memnon *see* Luxor
Coloured Canyon, Sinai 12, **165**
Common Starfish **157**
conservation projects 15
Constantine, Emperor 21
Constantinople (Istanbul) 21
Contemporary Egyptian Art Group 31
Coptic art 31, **158**
Coptic Christianity 17, 18, **18**, 21, 37, **46**, 61, **74-5**, **84**, **116**, **158**
Coptic Museum, Cairo 37
coral reefs 15, **15**, 151, **154**, **156**
coral species 15, **156**, **157**
Corban Bairam festival **133**
costume **16**, **78**, 129, **134**, 151, **162**, **166**
cotton growing 26, 31, 61, **64**
cows **139**
crafts 31-4, **33**, **87**, **142**, 151
crocodiles *see* Nile Crocodile
Cromer, Evelyn Baring, Lord 24
the Crusades 22, 23, **170**
cultural identity 16, 17, 18, 29, **29**, 125, 129, 132, **139**, **160**
cuttlefish 15

Dahshur:
  Bent Pyramid 30
Dakhlah 18, 129, **130**, **142**, **144-5**, **176**
Damietta (town) **67**
Damietta river 12
dance *see* music and dance
Daraw **110-11**
date palms 129, **138**, **149**
decorative motifs **18**, **22**, 23, 29, 30, **31**, 32, 33, 34, **38**, **49**, **51**, **53**, **87**, **90**, **97**, **117**, **138**, **142**, **149**
Deir Abu Maqar, Wadi al-Natrun **75**
Deir al-Abyad *see* White Monastery
Deir al-Ahmar *see* Red Monastery
Deir Anba Baramus, Wadi al-Natrun **75**
Deir Anba Bishoy, Wadi al-Natrun **62**, **74-5**

see also Red Monastery
Deir Anba Shenudah *see* White Monastery
Deir al-Bahri 20
Deir al-Suryan, Wadi al-Natrun **75**
Dendarah 77, **87**
  Chapel of the New Year **87**
  Hypostyle Hall **87**
  Temple of Hathor **87**
Dendronephthya coral **157**
desert areas 11, 12-13, 14, **14**, 15, 16-17, 61, **74-5**, 77, **94**, **110**, **115**, **121**, 129, **130-50**, **165**
Desert Fathers **159**
Desert Lynx *see* Caracal
Desert Rats 15
Diocletian, Emperor 17, **21**
diving and snorkelling 15, **15**, 151, **152**, **154-7**
dog family 15
dolphins 15, **156**, **157**
donkeys 14, **79**, **134**, **144**
ducks 14
Dugong 15

Eastern Desert 13, 151, **152**
economic conditions 23, 24, 25, 26
Edfu 21, 32, **109**
  Court of Offerings **109**
  Hypostyle Hall **109**
  Temple of Horus **109**
education and training 17, 22, 29, **32**, **84**
egrets 14
Egyptian Jerboas 15
Egyptian Museum, Cairo 31, 37, **105**
Egyptian Vulture 15
Egyptian Wild Cat 15
Egyptian-Israeli war, 1967 18
Eilat 25, 27
electricity supplies 13, 27, **121**, **130**
Elephantine Island, Aswan 17, 107, **122-5**
  Abu remains **122**
  Aswan Oberoi Hotel **122**
embroidery 151
Emperor Angelfish **154**
environmental issues **15**, **121**
Ethiopia 12
Euclid 72
European influences 18, 22-4, 29, 33, 61, **71**, **73**, **160**
Eurasian Spoonbill 14
exports 27

Fahmy, Azza 32
Fahmy, Ranada 32
Fairy Basslet **154**
Farafrah 129, **140**, **142**
Faruk, King 24-5
Fathy, Hassan **103**
Fatimid dynasty 22
Faud, King 24
fauna 14-15, **14**
Fayyum 14, 20, **27**, 77, **77-81**
fellaheen farmers 12, 16, 23, 24, **78**, **94**, **95**, **122**
felucca boats **6**, **10**, 12, 17, **89**, 107, **113**, **115**
Fennec **14**, 15

ferries **95**, 107, **160**
festivals 11, 29, **29**, 46, 61, **64-5**, 129, **132-4**, **165**
fire coral 15
fish species 14, 15, 34, **56**, **154**, **156**
fishing **13**, 62, 71, **73**, 77, **113**, **121**, **152**
flooding 12
flowers 32, **32**, 81
food and drink 34-5, **34-5**, 54, **56-7**, **89**, **125**, **133**, **134**,146
food supplies 13, 25, 27, **55**, **56**, **57**, 61
foreign investment 25, 26, 28, 66
Fort Qayt Bay, Alexandria **71**
Forty-Day Road **110**
foxes 15
France 18, 23, 25, 28
fuel supplies 13
Fustat 22, 37, **51**
Fuwah 61, 62

galabiyya robes **16**
Galal House, Rosetta **68**
Ganzouri, Kamel 26
Gaza 24, 25
gazelles 15
al-Gazzar, Abdel Hadi 31
geographical survey **8-9**, 11, 12-13
geological features 129, **137**
Giza 12, **40**, **44**
  Great Pyramids 18, 28, 30, 37, **38**, **40**, 81
  Khufu Pyramid **19**, **38**, **40**
  Qar temple **40**
  Queen's Pyramids **38**
  Sphinx **28**, 37, **38**, **40**
  Valley Temple **38**
glassblowing 32
Glassfish **157**
Glossy Ibis 14
goats **145**, **166**
gods 15, 19, 20, **82**, **86**, **87**, **90**, **92**, **97**, **98**, **104**
gold 13
gold and silversmiths 18, 32
Golden Oriole 14
Goniopora coral 15
gorgonian sea fans 15
government system 19, 25-6
Great Crested Grebe 14
Great Sand Sea **128**, **137**, **138**
Greater Flamingo 14
Greece 21, 30
Grey Shark 15, **157**
groupers 15
Gulf of Aqabah 13, 15, **15**, 151, **154**, **157**
Gulf Conflict, 1991 25, 26, 28
Gulf of Suez 13, 28, **154**, **157**, **158**

Hafez, Abd el-Halim 29
hageen racing camels **169**
Hammerhead Shark 15, **157**
el-Hamuli, Abdu 29
Haqqi, Yahya 28
Haroeris **109**
Hathor **87**, **97**, **165**
Hatshepsut, Queen 20, **30**, **97**
hawks 15

INDEX

Hawksbill Turtle 15, **156**
Haykal, Muhammad Hussein 28
herons 14
Hibis **149**
hieroglyphs 18, 61, **69**, **92**, **104**
historical survey 12, 13, 14, 15, 16, 17-18, 19-25, **81**, **139**, **142**, 151, **152**
horses 14, **169**
Horus 19, **104**, **109**
houseboats 47
Hurghadah 13, 151, **152**, **154**
Hussein, Taha 28
hydroelectric power 13, 27, **121**
Hyksos rulers 20

ibis 14
Ibn Tulun 22
Ibn Tulun Mosque, Cairo **22**, 30, 37, **51**
Idris, Yusuf 28
Ikhshidid dynasty 22
Imhotep 19, **41**
imports 27
Indian Ocean 12, **66**
industrial development 26-7
international relations 23, 24-5
Iran 25
Iraq 13, 25, 26
irrigation projects 12, 13, **13**, 27, **27**, 62, 77, **78**, **79**, **122**, **145**, **146**
Islam 17, **17**, 18, **18**, **22**, 28, **38**, **45**, **47**, **48**, **117**, **139**, **142**, **173**
 fundamentalists 17, 25, 28, 29
Islamic art **18**, **22**, **29**, 30, **31**, 32, 33, **38**, **49**, **51**, **53**, **117**, **142**
Islamic Empire 21-2
Ismailiyyah 26, **160**
Israel 12, 18, 24-5, 26, 27, 151, **160**, **162**

Jabalyyah tribe **166**
jackals 15
jacks **157**
al-jeel music 29
Jerboa **14**, 15
Jerusalem 22
jewellery 32, 129, 151, **162**
Jordan 13
Judaism 18, 21, 37, **173**

Kaffir Cat *see* Egyptian Wild Cat
Karnak 20, 77, **90**, **92**
 Hypostyle Hall **92**
 Great Temple of Amun 20, **92**
 Temple of Ptah **92**
khamsin winds 14
Khargah Oasis 129, **146**, **149**
kharsif bricks **130**
Kiosk of Qirtasi, Aswan **121**
Kolthum, Om 29
Kom Ombo 21, **109**, **110**, **125**
Koran 29, 44, **67**
Kuwait 25, 26

Lake Burullus 61
Lake Nasser 13, 14, 17, 34, 107, **121**, **122**, **126**
 see also Aswan Dam
languages 17, 18, 20, 129
Lanner Falcon 15
Lebanon 13, 22
Libya 12, 17, 21, 26, 129
Libyan desert 12
limestone monoliths 129, **140**

literature 28
Little Green Bee-Eater 14
local government 26
Lower Egypt 12, 19, 20
Luxor (Thebes) **6**, 19, 20-21, 77, **88-91**, **94**, **97-106**, 107
 Asasif Tombs **99**
 Aten shrine **90**
 Chapel of Hathor **97**
 Colossi of Memnon 20, 30, 77, **97**
 Madinat Habu **97**, **99**
 Mortuary Tomb of Queen Hatshepsut 30, **97**, **99**
 obelisks **90**
 Place of Truth **99**
 Ramesses II Colossi 30, **78**, **90**
 Ramesseum 30, **97**
 Sphinx avenue **90**
 temple complex 20, 30, 77, **78**, **90**
 Tomb of Ramose **101**
 Tomb of Sennedjem **99**
 Tomb of Sennufer **101**
 Tomb of the steward Kheru-ef **99**
 Tombs of the Nobles and Queens **101**
 Workmen's tombs **99**
Luxor Museum of Ancient Egyptian Art **90**

Madinat al-Maadi, Fayyum **81**
Mahfouz, Naguib 28
Mamluks 22-4, 30, 33, 34, 129
mammal species 14, 15
marine life 15, **15**, 151, **154-7**
markets **5**, **33**, 35, **35**, **54-7**, **71**, **103**, 107, **110-11**, **125**, 151, **160**, **162**
Marsh Sandpiper 14
mausoleums **31**, 37, **49**, 107, **115**, **117**, **149**, **152**
Maydum:
 Collapsed Pyramid 30, 77, **81**
Medinet Ma'adi:
 temples 77
Mediterranean Sea 11, 12, 13, 14, 34, **35**, 61, **66**, **71**, 162
Memphis 19, 20, 37, **43**, **86**
metalwork 32, **58**
Middle Egypt 19, 77, **82-5**
Middle Kingdom 19-20, 107
mining industry 13, **152**
Monasteries of St Paul and St Anthony *see* Red Sea Monasteries
Mongols 23
mongooses 15
monuments 19-20, 29, **40**, 77
moray eels 15
Morocco 29
Morsi, Abdel Wahab 31
mosques 17, 22, **22**, 23, 30, 37, **48**, **49**, **51**, **53**, **73**, **103**, **129**, **132**, **142**
Moulid of Sayyid Ahmad al-Badawi **64**
moulids see festivals
al-Muayyad Mosque, Cairo **51**, **53**
Mubarak, Husni, President 25, 26
muezzins 17, 29
Muhammad Ali 23-4, 37, **48**, **71**, 129
Muhammad Ali Mosque, Cairo 37, **48**
mules 14

mummies 82, **98**
munshids 29
Murad, Leila 29
murals 87, **98**, **99**, **101**, **104**, **105**, **109**, **117**, **158**
music and dance 29, **29**, **98**
Muslim Brotherhood 24
Muslims *see* Islam
Mut, Dakhlah Oasis 129, **142**, **144-5**, **176**
myths and legends 19, 20, **86**

Nada, Hamdi 31
Naghi, Muhammad 31
Napoleon, Emperor 23, 29
Napoleon Wrasse 15
Nassar, Wahib 31
al-Nasser, Gamal Abd, President 13, 25
national parks 15, **156**
nationalist forces 24-5, **72**
natural gas 13, 27
natural resources 13, 26, 27
Necropolis of al-Baqawat, Khargah **149**
Nefertari, Queen **126**
Nefertiti, Queen 20, 31
New Kingdom 20-21, 30, 77, **87**, **90**, **97**, **104**
New Qurnah *see* Qurnah
Nile Crocodile 14-15
Nile Delta 12, 14, 16, 19, **25**, 26, 27, 30, 61, **62-76**
Nile Perch 14
Nile river **6**, **10**, 12, 13, **13**, 14-15, 16, 19, 27, **44**, 77, **78-106**, 151, **152**
 New Valley 27, 129, **146**
 Roda Island 44
 see also Aswan
Nilometers 44
nomadic peoples 16, 77, **110-11**, 151, **162**, **165-7**
North African Arabs 17
Northern Oasis *see* Bahriyyah Oasis
Nubia 17, 20, 21
Nubian desert 12
Nubian Museum, Aswan **116**
Nubian people **16**, 17, 20, 29, 107, **121-5**

oases 12, 16, 18, 129, **130-35**, **138-9**, **142-9**, **152**, **166**
octopus 15
oil supplies 13, 26, 27
oil transportation 27-8
Old Kingdom 19, **43**, **86**, 107
olive groves **138**
Oracle of Amun 129
Osiris 19, **86**, **98**
Ottoman Empire **16**, 23
owls 15

painting **20**, 30-31, **53**, **98**, **99**, **101**
Palestine 22, 24, 25, 32
Palette of King Narmer 30
papyrus sheets 18, 33
parliamentary system 25
Parrotfish 15
perfume industry 32, **55**
Persia 21, 29
Pharaonic Dynasties 19-21, 30, 37, 77
Pharos lighthouse, Alexandria 61, **71**
the Phoenicians 32
Pied Kingfisher 14
pigeons 35, **57**
plankton 15
political parties 25, 26

Pompey's Pillar, Alexandria **21**
population density 12, 16, 27, 37, **45**, **73**, **146**
Porites coral 15
Port Said 12, **24**, 25, 26, 61, **66**
power supplies 13
precious stones 13
pyramids 19, **19**, 20-21, **38**, **81**

al-Qahirah 22
Qantarah **160**
Al-Qasr, Daklah Oasis **18**, 129, **129**, **142**
Al-Qasr al-Farafrah **142**
Qasr al-Ghuwaydah temple, Khargah **149**
Qattarah Depression **130**
Qift **152**
al-Qitai 22
al-Qurnah **102-3**
 New Qurnah 77, **103**
Al-Qusayr **152**, **154**

rainfall 12, 14
Ramadan 17
Ramesses I, *Pharoah* **104**
Ramesses II, *Pharoah* 21, 30, **43**, **78**, **90**, **97**, **126**
Ramesses III, *Pharoah* **97**
Ramesses VI, *Pharoah* **104**
Ras Abu Galum 15
Ras Muhammed National Park 15, **156**
al-Rashid, Harun 28
Red Monastery, Sohag 77, **84**
Red Mosque *see* Sultan Hassan Mosque, Cairo
Red Sea 12, **12**, 13, 15, **15**, 151, **152**, **154-7**
Red Sea Monasteries 18, 30, 151, **158-9**
Red Sea Mountains 13, 151, **152**
Red-tailed Catfish 14
reef fish 15
religious beliefs 17-18, 20, 21, 30-31, **92**
religious books **104**
Revolutionary Command Council (RCC) 25
Rock Hyrax **14**, 15
Rocky Island, Red Sea **154**
Roman Monastery *see* Deir Anba Baramus
Romans 21, 30, **149**
Rosetta (town) **16**, **31**, 61, **68**, **69**
Rosetta river 12
Rosetta Stone 61, **69**

el-Saadawi, Nawal 28
Sabil-Kuttab of Ruqwuyyah Dudu, Cairo **53**
el-Sadat, Anwar, President 25, 26
Saharan desert 12, 14
Said, Mahmud 31
St Bishoy Church *see* Deir Anba Bishoy (Red Monastery)
St Catherine's Monastery, Sinai 17, 151, **166**, **170-73**
 Steps of Repentance **172**
St Shenute Monastery *see* White Monastery
St Simeon's Monastery, Aswan 30, 107, **115**
Salah al-Din (Saladin) 22, 37
Sand Cat 15
sand dunes **128**, 129, **137**
Saqqarah **42-3**

catacombs 14, **41**, **43**
Colossus of Ramesses II **43**
Kagemni tomb **43**
Mastaba of Ti **42**
Step Pyramid 19, **19**, 30, 37, **38**, **41**
Sarabit al-Khadim **165**
schools 22, 29, **84**
scorpions 15
sculpture **20**, 30-31
sea defences 12
sea fans **157**
Sekhmet **92**
Semitic peoples 16, **16**
Serri, Gazbia 31
Seti I, Pharoah 21, **105**
Seven Wonders of the Ancient World 20, 30, 77, **97**
shaabi music 29
Shali, Siwah Oasis **131**
shark species 15, **156**, **157**
Sharm al-Shaykh 151, **156**
sheep **62**, **63**, **145**, **166**
sheesha water-pipes 35, **55**, **89**
Shining Sunbird 14
Sinai (Mount) 13, 18, **150**, 151, **170**, **172**
Sinai Peninsula 12, 13, 15, 16, 25, **29**, 30, 34, **35**, 151, **151**, **160-75**
Siwah Oasis 17, 129, **130-35**, **137**, **138**
Siwan people 129
snakes 15
snappers 15
Sobek **109**
Sohag 18, 77, **84**
soil erosion 12
Solar Barque **19**
Spider Crabs **157**
spiky elkhorn coral 15
squid 15
starfish species **157**
statues and Colossi 20, 30, **40**, **42**, **43**, 77, **90**, **92**, **97**
stelae **165**
stingrays 15
Straits of Gubal 151
Straits of Tiran **156**
street vendors 34-5, **35**, **146**
Stylophora coral 15
Sudan 12, 16, 107, **110**, **121**
Suez 12, 26
Suez Canal 12, 13, **13**, 24-5, 27-8, 61, **66**, 151, **160**
Suez Crisis, 1956 18
Suez-Mediterranean (Sumed) pipeline 28
Sufi Muslims 29, **64**
sulphur springs **144**
Sultan Hassan Mosque, Cairo 37, **51**
Sultan Qayt-bay Mausoleum, Cairo **31**, 37
Sunni Muslims 17
Surgeonfish 15
Syria 13, 22, 23, 25, 32

al-Tabarna Mosque, Alexandria **73**
Tanta **25**, **64-5**
Tell al-Amarnah 20
temperature range 14
Temple of Amun, Khargah **149**
Temple of Hathor, Sarabit al-Khadim **165**
Temple of Isis, Philae Island, Aswan 107, **118**
 Kiosk of Trajan **118**
 Lion Statue **118**
temples 30, **38**, **41**, 77, 87, **90**, **92**, **98**, 107, **109**, **126**, **149**

175

This is Egypt

tent-making 31, **58**
tents **166**
textile industry 26-7, 31-2, **32**, 61, **63**
Theban Triad 20, **90**
Thebes *see* Luxor
The Thousand-and-One Nights 28
Tilapia 14
Tiran Island, Red Sea **156**
tomb robbers **102**
tombs 19, 20, **30**, 31, 32, 37, **38**, **42**, **43**, 77, **82**, **98**, **104-5**, 107
Tombs of the Nobles, Aswan 107
tourism 26, 28, **28**, 29, 61, **88**, **95**, **102**, 107, **140**, **146**, 151, **152**, **165**

trade links 12, **13**, 21, 23, 24, 27, **66**, **67**, 72, **152**, **160**
traditional life 11, 12, 17, 29, **29**, 35, **46**, **47**, 49, 55, **62**, **63**, **67**, **89**, **94**, **95**, **99**, **101**, 107, **131-2**, **143-5**
transport and communications 12, 14, **47**, **63**, **67**, **68**, **79**, **95**, 107, **110**, **134**, **144**, **160**, **165**
Tunah al-Gabal **82**
Turkey 13, **16**, 22, 24, 27, 33
Tutankhamun, *Pharoah* 20, 21, **90**
  death mask 31, 32, **105**
  tomb 32, 37, **105**
Tuthmosis I, *Pharoah* 20
Tuthmosis II, *Pharoah* 20, **90**

UNESCO **118**
United Arab Republic (UAR) 25
United Nations 25
universities 17, 22
Upper Egypt 19, 21, 26, 77
USA 25, 26
USSR 13, 25

Valley of the Kings 20, 77, **88**, **98**, **99**, **102**, **104-5**
  Ramesses I tomb **104**
  Ramesses VI tomb **104**
  Seti I tomb **105**
  Tutankhamun tomb 31, 32, 37, **105**
Valley of the Queens 77, **101**
  murals **101**
  Tomb of Nefertari 31, 77

Wadi Halfa **121**
Wadi al-Natrun 61, 77
  monasteries **4**, 18, 30, 61, **62**, **74-5**
wadis **12**, 13, **165**, **169**
wall hangings 34
Wassef, Ramses Wissa 34
water birds 14
water supplies 12, 13, **131**, **146**, 151, **169**
water wheels **27**, 77, **79**
weaving industry 27, 33-4
West Bank **97-106**, **115**, **122**, **125**
Western Desert 12-13, **14**, 16, 17, 18, 129, **130-50**
Western Empire 21
wetlands 61
whale sharks 15

whirling dervishes 29
White Desert 129, **140**, **142**
White Monastery, Sohag 77, **84**
Whitetip Sharks 15
wild dogs 15
wild geese 14
wildlife *see* fauna
wine and beer 35
women **16**, 17, 28, 29, **45**, **58**, **78**, 129, **133**, **151**, **162**, **166**, **176**
wool trade **62**, **63**
wrecks 151, **156**

Xeniid soft coral 15

Zanatah Berbers 17
Zozer, King 19, **19**, **41**, **81**

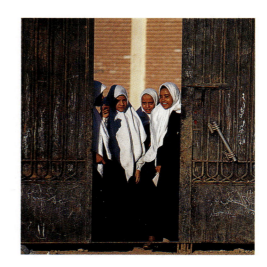